LUCIFER—
HOW ART THOU FALLEN?

By
Ellen G. White

TEACH Services, Inc.

Copyright © 2007 TEACH Services, Inc.
ISBN-13: 978-1-57258-475-4
Library of Congress Control Number: 2007926709

Published by

TEACH Services, Inc.
www.TEACHServices.com

CONTENTS

Chapter 1

LUCIFER AT CREATION

It was a being of wonderful power and glory that had set himself against God. Of Lucifer the Lord says, "Thou sealest up the sum, full of wisdom, and perfect in beauty." Ezek. 28:12. Lucifer had been the covering cherub. He had stood in the light of God's presence. He had been the highest of all created beings, and had been foremost in revealing God's purposes to the universe. After he had sinned, his power to deceive was the more deceptive, and the unveiling of his character was the more difficult, because of the exalted position he had held with the Father. *Desire of Ages*, 758.

So long as all created beings acknowledged the allegiance of love, there was perfect harmony throughout the universe of God. It was the joy of the heavenly host to fulfill the purpose of their Creator. They delighted in reflecting His glory and showing forth His praise. And while love to God was supreme, love for one another was confiding and unselfish. There was no note of discord to mar the celestial harmonies…[Lucifer], next to Christ, had been most honored of God and was highest in power and glory among the inhabitants of heaven. Lucifer, "son of the morning," was first of the covering cherubs, holy and undefiled. He stood in the presence of the great Creator, and the ceaseless beams of glory enshrouding the eternal God rested upon him. *Patriarchs and Prophets*, 35.

He had been made beautiful, he had been highly exalted in heaven, and his heart was lifted up because of his beauty; he had corrupted his wisdom by reason of his brightness. Of him it had been said: "Thou sealest up the sum, full of wisdom, and perfect in beauty. Thou hast been in Eden the garden of God; every precious stone was thy covering, the sardius, topaz, and the diamond, the beryl, the onyx, and

1

the jasper, the sapphire, the emerald, and the carbuncle, and gold....Thou art the anointed cherub that covereth; and I have set thee so; thou wast upon the holy mountain of God; thou hast walked up and down in the midst of the stones of fire. Thou wast perfect in thy ways from the day that thou wast created, till iniquity was found in thee." *Signs of the Times*, 9-24-94.

Satan in heaven, before his rebellion, was a high and exalted angel, next in honor to God's dear Son. His countenance, like those of the other angels, was mild and expressive of happiness. His forehead was high and broad, showing a powerful intellect. His form was perfect; his bearing noble and majestic. A special light beamed in his countenance, and shone around him brighter and more beautiful than around the other angels; yet Jesus, God's dear Son, had the pre-eminence over all the angelic host. He was one with the Father before the angels were created. Satan was envious of Christ, and in his ambition assumed command which devolved on Christ alone. *Signs of the Times*, 1-9-79.

Sin originated with him, who, next to Christ, stood highest in the favor of God, and highest in power and glory among the inhabitants of Heaven. Before his fall, Lucifer was the covering cherub, holy and undefiled. The prophet of God declares, "Thou wast perfect in thy ways from the day that thou wast created, till iniquity was found in thee."[1 EZE. 28:15.] Peace and joy, in perfect submission to the will of Heaven, existed throughout the angelic host. Love to God was supreme, love for one another impartial. Such was the condition that existed for ages before the entrance of sin.

...Though God had created Lucifer noble and beautiful, and had exalted him to high honor among the angelic host, yet he had not placed him beyond the possibility of evil. It was in Satan's power, did he choose to do so, to pervert these gifts. He might have remained in favor with God, beloved and honored by all the angelic throng, presiding in his exalted position with generous, unselfish care, exercising his noble powers to bless others and to glorify his Maker...*The Spirit of Prophecy*, Volume Four, 316, 317.

The Gospel is the voice of duty and the voice of God. What is meant by a failure to obey its principles is shown in the history of Satan, who for his disobedience was cast out of heaven. The highest gifts that could be bestowed in a created being were given to Lucifer, the covering cherub. Before his fall he was a glorious being, occupying a position next to Christ in the heavenly courts. But in seeking to be equal with God he brought upon himself irretrievable ruin. *The Signs of the Times*, 7-10-01.

Chapter 2

LUCIFER'S PRIDE

It is only by a clear discernment of spiritual things that the original apostasy can be understood. The controversy in heaven began with selfish strife for position, a desire on the part of Lucifer to be equal with God. The disaffection of Satan in entertaining the thought that he should stand as head of the heavenly order at first seemed a small thing, but by dwelling upon this thought, it was strengthened. Step by step he miscalculated the position that had been assigned him by God, to be maintained only in God, until he finally came to look with enmity upon everything coming from Jesus Christ. Satan rebelled against the laws governing the heavenly intelligences; and by representing these in a deceptive light, by his unbelief and complaints, he drew others with him into rebellion. *Advent Review and Sabbath Herald*, 5-30-99.

Little by little Lucifer came to indulge the desire for self-exaltation. The Scripture says, "Thine heart was lifted up because of thy beauty, thou hast corrupted thy wisdom by reason of thy brightness." Ezekiel 28:17. "Thou hast said in thine heart,...I will exalt my throne above the stars of God.... I will be like the Most High." Isaiah 14:13, 14. Though all his glory was from God, this mighty angel came to regard it as pertaining to himself. Not content with his position, though honored above the heavenly host, he ventured to covet homage due alone to the Creator. Instead of seeking to make God supreme in the affections and allegiance of all created beings, it was his endeavor to secure their service and loyalty to himself. And coveting the glory with which the infinite Father had invested His Son, this prince of angels aspired to power that was the prerogative of Christ alone.

Now the perfect harmony of heaven was broken. Lucifer's disposition to serve himself instead of his Creator aroused a

feeling of apprehension when observed by those who consid-
ered that the glory of God should be supreme...Lucifer allowed his jealousy of Christ to prevail, and became the more
determined. *Patriarchs and Prophets*, 35, 36.

The angels joyfully acknowledged the supremacy of
Christ, and prostrating themselves before Him, poured out
their love and adoration. Lucifer bowed with them, but in
his heart there was a strange, fierce conflict. Truth, justice,
and loyalty were struggling against envy and jealousy. The
influence of the holy angels seemed for a time to carry him
with them. As songs of praise ascended in melodious strains,
swelled by thousands of glad voices, the spirit of evil seemed
vanquished; unutterable love thrilled his entire being; his
soul went out, in harmony with the sinless worshippers, in
love to the Father and the Son. But again he was filled with
pride in his own glory. His desire for supremacy returned,
and envy of Christ was once more indulged. The high honors conferred upon Lucifer were not appreciated as God's
special gift, and therefore, called forth no gratitude to his
Creator. He glorified in his brightness and exaltation and aspired to be equal with God. He was beloved and reverenced
by the heavenly host, angels delighted to execute his commands, and he was clothed with wisdom and glory above
them all. Yet the Son of God was exalted above him, as one in
power and authority with the Father. He shared the Father's
counsels, while Lucifer did not thus enter into the purposes
of God. "Why," questioned this mighty angel, "should Christ
have the supremacy? Why is He honored above Lucifer?"

Leaving his place in the immediate presence of the Father, Lucifer went forth to diffuse the spirit of discontent
among the angels. He worked with mysterious secrecy, and
for a time concealed his real purpose under an appearance
of reverence for God. He began to insinuate doubts concerning the laws that governed heavenly beings, intimating that
though laws might be necessary for the inhabitants of the
worlds, angels, being more exalted, needed no such restraint,
for their own wisdom was a sufficient guide. They were not
beings that could bring dishonor to God; all their thoughts

were holy; it was no more possible for them than for God Himself to err. The exaltation of the Son of God as equal with the Father was represented as an injustice to Lucifer, who, it was claimed, was also entitled to reverence and honor. If this prince of angels could but attain to his true, exalted position, great good would accrue to the entire host of heaven; for it was his object to secure freedom for all. But now even the liberty which they had hitherto enjoyed was at an end; for an absolute Ruler had been appointed them, and to His authority all must pay homage. Such were the subtle deceptions that through the wiles of Lucifer were fast obtaining in the heavenly courts. *Patriarchs and Prophets*, 36.

Pride in his own glory nourished the desire for supremacy. The high honors conferred upon Lucifer were not appreciated as the gift of God and called forth no gratitude to the Creator. He gloried in his brightness and exaltation, and aspired to be equal with God. He was beloved and reverenced by the heavenly host. Angels delighted to execute his commands, and he was clothed with wisdom and glory above them all. Yet the Son of God was the acknowledged Sovereign of heaven, one in power and authority with the Father. In all the councils of God, Christ was a participant, while Lucifer was not permitted thus to enter into the divine purposes. "Why," questioned this mighty angel, "should Christ have the supremacy? Why is He thus honored above Lucifer?" *The Great Controversy*, 495.

But though honored above the heavenly host, Lucifer was not content with his position. He ventured to covet the homage due alone to the Creator. He cherished feelings of envy, and these feelings he communicated to the other angels. It was his endeavor to secure to himself their service and loyalty. In so deceptive a way did he [Lucifer] work that the sentiments that he inculcated could not be dealt with until they had developed in the minds of those who received them. *Manuscript Releases*, Vol. 7, 63.

Evil originated with Lucifer, who rebelled against the government of God. Before his fall he was a covering cherub, distinguished by his excellence. God made him good and beautiful, as near as possible like himself. Of him it is written, "Thou wast perfect in thy ways from the day that thou wast created, till iniquity was found in thee." But self-exaltation entered his heart. Inspiration records the charge against him: "Thine heart wast lifted up because of thy beauty, thou hast corrupted thy wisdom by reason of thy brightness." "How art thou fallen from heaven, O Lucifer, son of the morning! how art thou cut down to the ground, which didst weaken the nations! For thou hast said in thine heart, I will ascend unto heaven, I will exalt my throne above the stars of God: I will sit also upon the mount of the congregation, in the sides of the north: I will ascend above the heights of the clouds; I will be like the Most High. Yet thou shalt be brought down to hell, to the sides of the pit." *Advent Review and Sabbath Herald*, 9-24-01.

Lucifer refused to accept Christ as the Prince of heaven, his Sovereign and Leader. He refused to acknowledge the supremacy of the Son of God. The controversy between the Prince of life and the prince of darkness has been long and fierce. Those who place themselves under Satan's banner, who refuse, as did the Jews, to yield allegiance to God or to obey His laws, can never be members of the heavenly family. They would make war against the law of Jehovah, calling it, as did Satan, a yoke of bondage. *Advent Review and Sabbath Herald*, 3-12-01.

The change from perfection of character to sin and defection did come even in heaven. Lucifer's heart was lifted up because of his beauty, his wisdom was corrupted by reason of his brightness. Self-exaltation is the key to his rebellion, and it unlocks the modern theme of sanctification. Satan declared that he had no need of the restraints of law, that he was holy, sinless, and incapable of doing evil; and those who boast of holiness and a state of sinlessness, while transgressing the law of God, while willfully trampling under-foot the

Sabbath of the Lord, are allied on the side of the first great rebel. If the sanctified, holy angels became unsanctified and unholy by disobedience to God's law, and their place was no longer found in heaven, think you that men, redeemed by the blood of the Lamb, will be received into glory who break the precepts of that law which Christ came to magnify and make honorable by his death upon the cross? Adam and Eve were in possession of Eden, and they fell from their high and holy estate by transgression of God's law, and forfeited their right to the tree of life and to the joys of Eden. *The Signs of the Times*, 4-28-90.

"Thou shalt have no other gods before me." Lucifer disputed the justice of this requirement in heaven, and thought its existence altogether unnecessary. He said in his heart: "I will ascend into heaven, I will exalt my throne above the stars of God; I will sit also upon the mount of the congregation, in the sides of the north; I will ascend above the heights of the clouds; I will be like the Most High." He had been made beautiful, he had been highly exalted in heaven, and his heart was lifted up because of his beauty; he had corrupted his wisdom by reason of his brightness. The *Signs of the Times*, 9-24-94.

The Saviour gathered His disciples about Him, and said to them, "If any man desire to be first, the same shall be last of all, and servant of all." There was in these words a solemnity and impressiveness which the disciples were far from comprehending. That which Christ discerned they could not see. They did not understand the nature of Christ's kingdom, and this ignorance was the apparent cause of their contention. But the real cause lay deeper. By explaining the nature of the kingdom, Christ might for the time have quelled their strife; but this would not have touched the underlying cause. Even after they had received the fullest knowledge, any question of precedence might have renewed the trouble. Thus disaster would have been brought to the church after Christ's departure. The strife for the highest place was the outworking of that same spirit which was the beginning of the great controversy in the worlds above, and which had brought Christ from heaven to die. There rose up before Him a vision of Lucifer, the "son of the morning," in glory surpassing all the angels that surround the throne, and united in closest ties to the Son of God. Lucifer had said, "I will be like the Most High" (Isa. 14:12, 14); and the desire for self-exaltation had brought strife into the heavenly courts, and had banished a multitude of the hosts of God. Had Lucifer really desired to be like the Most High, he would never have deserted his appointed place in heaven; for the spirit of the Most High is manifested in unselfish ministry. Lucifer desired God's power, but not His character. He sought for himself the highest place, and every being who is actuated by his spirit will do the same. Thus alienation, discord, and strife will be inevitable. Dominion becomes the prize of the strongest. The kingdom of Satan is a kingdom of force; every individual regards every other as an obstacle in the way of his own advancement, or a steppingstone on which he himself may climb to a higher place. *The Desire of Ages*, 435, 436.

Chapter 3

LUCIFER WARNED

In great mercy, according to His divine character, God bore long with Lucifer. The spirit of discontent and disaffection had never before been known in heaven. It was a new element, strange, mysterious, unaccountable. Lucifer himself had not at first been acquainted with the real nature of his feelings; for a time he had feared to express the workings and imaginings of his mind; yet he did not dismiss them. He did not see whither he was drifting. But such efforts as infinite love and wisdom only could devise, were made to convince him of his error. His disaffection was proved to be without cause, and he was made to see what would be the result of persisting in revolt. Lucifer was convinced that he was in the wrong. He saw that "the Lord is righteous in all His ways, and holy in all His works" (Psalm 145:17); that the divine statutes are just, and that he ought to acknowledge them as such before all heaven. Had he done this, he might have saved himself and many angels. He had not at that time fully cast off his allegiance to God. Though he had left his position as covering cherub, yet if he had been willing to return to God, acknowledging the Creator's wisdom, and satisfied to fill the place appointed him in God's great plan, he would have been reinstated in his office. The time had come for a final decision; he must fully yield to the divine sovereignty or place himself in open rebellion. He nearly reached the decision to return, but pride forbade him. It was too great a sacrifice for one who had been so highly honored to confess that he had been in error, that his imaginings were false, and to yield to the authority which he had been working to prove unjust.

A compassionate Creator, in yearning pity for Lucifer and his followers, was seeking to draw them back from the abyss of ruin into which they were about to plunge. But His mercy was misinterpreted. Lucifer pointed to the long-suffering of God as an evidence of his own superiority, an indication that the King of the universe would yet accede to his terms. If the angels would stand firmly with him, he declared, they could yet gain all that they desired. He persistently defended his own course, and fully committed himself to the great controversy against his Maker. Thus it was that Lucifer, "the light bearer," the sharer of God's glory, the attendant of His throne, by transgression became Satan, "the adversary" of God and holy beings and the destroyer of those whom Heaven had committed to his guidance and guardianship. *Patriarchs and Prophets*, 39, 40.

The heavenly councils admonished Lucifer to change his course. The Son of God warned and entreated him not to venture thus to dishonor his Maker, and bring ruin upon himself. But instead of yielding, Satan represented to those who loved him, that he had been wrongly judged, that his dignity was not respected, and that his liberty was to be abridged. *The Spirit of Prophecy*, Volume Four, 317.

He was not immediately dethroned when he first ventured to indulge the spirit of discontent and insubordination, nor even when he began to present his false claim and lying representations before the loyal angels. Long was he retained in Heaven. Again and again was he offered pardon on condition of repentance and submission. Such efforts as God alone could make, were made to convince him of his error, and restore him to the path of rectitude. God would preserve the order of the heavens, and had Lucifer been willing to return to his allegiance, humble and obedient, he would have been re-established in his office as covering cherub. *The Spirit of Prophecy*, Volume Four, 319, 320.

Rejecting with disdain the arguments and entreaties of the loyal angels, he denounced them as deluded slaves. The preference shown to Christ he declared an act of injustice both to himself and to all the heavenly host, and announced that he would no longer submit to this invasion of his rights and theirs. He would never again acknowledge the supremacy of Christ. He had determined to claim the honor which should have been given him, and take command of all who would become his followers; and he promised those would enter his ranks a new and better government, under which all would enjoy freedom. Great numbers of the angels signified their purpose to accept him as their leader. Flattered by the favor with which his advances were received, he hoped to win all the angels to his side, to become equal with God Himself, and to be obeyed by the entire host of heaven.

Still the loyal angels urged him and his sympathizers to submit to God; and they set before them the inevitable result should they refuse: He who had created them could overthrow their power and signally punish their rebellious daring. No angel could successfully oppose the law of God, which was as sacred as Himself. They warned all to close their ears against Lucifer's deceptive reasoning, and urged him and his followers to seek the presence of God without delay and confess the error of questioning His wisdom and authority. *Patriarchs and Prophets*, 40.

All heaven had rejoiced to reflect the Creator's glory and to show forth His praise. And while God was thus honored, all had been peace and gladness. But a note of discord now marred the celestial harmonies. The service and exaltation of self, contrary to the Creator's plan, awakened forebodings of evil in minds to whom God's glory was supreme. The heavenly councils pleaded with Lucifer. The Son of God presented before him the greatness, the goodness, and the justice of the Creator, and the sacred, unchanging nature of His law. God Himself had established the order of heaven; and in departing from it, Lucifer would dishonor his Maker, and bring ruin upon himself. But the warning, given in infinite love and mercy, only aroused a spirit of resistance. Lucifer allowed jealousy of Christ to prevail, and he became the more determined. *The Great Controversy*, 494.

Chapter 4

LUCIFER'S INFLUENCE

There had been no change in the position or authority of Christ. Lucifer's envy and misrepresentation and his claims to equality with Christ had made necessary a statement of the true position of the Son of God; but this had been the same from the beginning. Many of the angels were, however, blinded by Lucifer's deceptions.

Taking advantage of the loving, loyal trust reposed in him by the holy beings under his command, he had so artfully instilled into their minds his own distrust and discontent that his agency was not discerned. Lucifer had presented the purposes of God in a false light—misconstruing and distorting them to excite dissent and dissatisfaction. He cunningly drew his hearers on to give utterance to their feelings; then these expressions were repeated by him when it would serve his purpose, as evidence that the angels were not fully in harmony with the government of God. While claiming for himself perfect loyalty to God, he urged that changes in the order and laws of heaven were necessary for the stability of the divine government. Thus while working to excite opposition to the law of God and to instill his own discontent into the minds of the angels under him, he was ostensibly seeking to remove dissatisfaction and to reconcile disaffected angels to the order of heaven. While secretly fomenting discord and rebellion, he with consummate craft caused it to appear as his sole purpose to promote loyalty and to preserve harmony and peace.

The spirit of dissatisfaction thus kindled was doing its baleful work. While there was no open outbreak, division of feeling imperceptibly grew up among the angels. There were some who looked with favor upon Lucifer's insinuations against the government of God. Although they had heretofore been in perfect harmony with the order which God had established, they were now discontented and unhappy because they could not penetrate His unsearchable counsels; they were dissatisfied with His purpose in exalting Christ. These stood ready to second Lucifer's demand for equal authority with the Son of God. But angels who were loyal and true maintained the wisdom and justice of he divine decree and endeavored to reconcile this disaffected being to the will of God. Christ was the Son of God; He had been one with Him before the angels were called into existence. He had ever stood at the right hand of the Father; His supremacy, so full of blessing to all who came under its benignant control, had not heretofore been questioned. The harmony of heaven had never been interrupted; wherefore should there now be discord? The loyal angels could see only terrible consequences from this dissension, and with earnest entreaty they counseled the disaffected ones to renounce their purpose and prove themselves loyal to God by fidelity to His government. *Patriarchs and Prophets*, 38.

The records of some are similar to that of the exalted angel who was given a position next to Jesus Christ in the heavenly courts. Lucifer was enshrouded with glory as the covering cherub. Yet this angel whom God had created, and entrusted with power, became desirous of being as God. He gained the sympathy of some of his associates by suggesting thoughts of criticism regarding the government of God. This evil seed was scattered in a most seducing manner; and after it had sprung up and taken root in the minds of many, he gathered the ideas that he himself had first implanted in the minds of others, and brought them before the highest order of angels as the thoughts of other minds against the government of God. Thus, by ingenious methods of his own devising, Lucifer introduced rebellion in heaven. *S.D.A. Bible Commentary*, Vol. 4, 1143.

Leaving his place in the immediate presence of God, Lucifer went forth to diffuse the spirit of discontent among the angels. Working with mysterious secrecy, and for a time concealing his real purpose under an appearance of reverence for God, he endeavored to excite dissatisfaction concerning the laws that governed heavenly beings, intimating that they imposed an unnecessary restraint. Since their natures were holy, he urged that the angels should obey the dictates of their own will. He sought to create sympathy for himself by representing that God had dealt unjustly with him in bestowing supreme honor upon Christ. He claimed that in aspiring to greater power and honor he was not aiming at self-exaltation, but was seeking to secure liberty for all the inhabitants of heaven, that by this means they might attain to a higher state of existence. *The Great Controversy*, 495.

This work of opposition to the law of God had its beginning in the courts of heaven, with Lucifer, the covering cherub. Satan determined to be first in the councils of heaven, and equal with God. He began his work of rebellion with the angels under his command, seeking to diffuse among them the spirit of discontent. And he worked in so deceptive a way that many of the angels were won to his allegiance before his purposes were fully known. Even the loyal angels could not fully discern his character, nor see to what his work was leading. When Satan had succeeded in winning many angels to his side, he took his cause to God, representing that it was the desire of the angels that he occupy the position that Christ held. *Selected Messages*, Book 1, 222.

Many of Lucifer's sympathizers were inclined to heed the counsel of the loyal angels and repent of their dissatisfaction and be again received to the confidence of the Father and His dear Son. The mighty revolter then declared that he was acquainted with God's law, and if he should submit to servile obedience, his honor would be taken from him. No more would he be entrusted with his exalted mission. He told them that himself and they also had now gone too far to go back, and he would brave the consequences, for to bow in servile worship to the Son of God he never would; that God would not forgive, and now they must assert their liberty and gain by force the position and authority which was not willingly accorded to them. *Lift Him Up*, 19.

The influence of mind on mind, so strong a power for good when sanctified, is equally strong for evil in the hands of those opposed to God. This power Satan used in his work of instilling evil into the minds of the angels, and he made it appear that he was seeking the good of the universe. As the anointed cherub, Lucifer had been highly exalted; he was greatly loved by the heavenly beings, and his influence over them was strong. Many of them listened to his suggestions and believed his words. "And there was war in heaven: Michael and His angels fought against the dragon; and the dragon fought and his angels, and prevailed not; neither was their place found any more in heaven" (Revelation 12:8). *Mind, Character, and Personality*, Volume 1, 23.

Many were disposed to heed this counsel, to repent of their disaffection, and seek to be again received into favor with the Father and His Son. But Lucifer had another deception ready. The mighty revolter now declared that the angels who had united with him had gone too far to return; that he was acquainted with the divine law, and knew that God would not forgive. He declared that all who should submit to the authority of Heaven would be stripped of their honor, degraded from their position. For himself, he was determined never again to acknowledge the authority of Christ. The only course remaining for him and his followers, he said, was to assert their liberty, and gain by force the rights which had not been willingly accorded them.

So far as Satan himself was concerned, it was true that he had now gone too far to return. But not so with those who had been blinded by his deceptions. To them the counsel and entreaties of the loyal angels opened a door of hope; and had they heeded the warning, they might have broken away from the snare of Satan. But pride, love for their leader, and the desire for unrestricted freedom were permitted to bear sway, and the pleadings of divine love and mercy were finally rejected.

God permitted Satan to carry forward his work until the spirit of disaffection ripened into active revolt. It was necessary for his plans to be fully developed, that their true nature and tendency might be seen by all. Lucifer, as the anointed cherub, had been highly exalted; he was greatly loved by the heavenly beings, and his influence over them was strong. God's government included not only the inhabitants of heaven, but of all the worlds that He had created; and Lucifer had concluded that if he could carry the angels of heaven with him in rebellion, he could carry also all the worlds. He had artfully presented his side of the question, employing sophistry and fraud to secure his objects. His power to deceive was very great. By disguising himself in a cloak of falsehood, he had gained an advantage. All his acts were so clothed with mystery that it was difficult to disclose to the angels the true nature of his work. Until fully developed, it could not be made to appear the evil thing it was; his disaffection would not be seen to be rebellion. Even the loyal angels could not fully discern his character or see to what his work was leading.

Lucifer had at first so conducted his temptations that he himself stood uncommitted. The angels whom he could not bring fully to his side, he accused of indifference to the interests of heavenly beings. The very work which he himself was doing, he charged upon the loyal angels. It was his policy to perplex with subtle arguments concerning the purposes of God. Everything that was simple he shrouded in mystery, and by artful perversion cast doubt upon the plainest statements of Jehovah. And his high position, so closely connected with the divine government, gave greater force to his representations. *Patriarchs and Prophets*, 40.

In so deceptive a way did he [Lucifer] work that the sentiments that he inculcated could not be dealt with until they had developed in the minds of those who received them. *S.D.A. Bible Commentary*, Vol. 7, 973.

Tho all his glory was from God, Lucifer came to regard it as pertaining to himself. Not content with his position, tho honored above the heavenly host, he ventured to covet homage due alone to the Creator. Leaving his place in the immediate presence of the Father, he went forth to diffuse the spirit of discontent among the angels. He worked with mysterious secrecy, and for a time concealed his real purpose under an appearance of reverence for God. He began to insinuate doubts concerning the laws that governed heavenly beings,—he declared were arbitrary, detrimental to the interests of the heavenly universe, and in need of change. Vital interests were at stake. Would Lucifer succeed in undermining confidence in God's law? Would he make so apparent these supposed defects in the law, that the inhabitants of the heavenly universe would be justified in claiming that the law could be improved? *Signs of the Times*, 7-23-02.

It was Satan's desire for supremacy that caused discord among the angels. The mighty Lucifer, "son of the morning," claimed the right to honor and authority above the Son of God; and this not being accorded him, he determined to rebel against the government of Heaven. He therefore appealed to the angelic host, complaining of God's injustice, and declaring himself deeply wronged. His false representations won to his side one-third of all the heavenly angels; and so strong was their delusion that they would not be corrected; they clung to Lucifer... *The Signs of the Times*, 10-25-83.

Chapter 5

LUCIFER SENTENCED

God in His wisdom permitted Satan to carry forward his work, until the spirit of disaffection ripened into active revolt. It was necessary for his plans to be fully developed, that their true nature and tendency might be seen by all. *Great Controversy*, 497.

The influence of mind on mind, so strong a power for good when sanctified, is equally strong for evil in the hands of those opposed to God. This power Satan used in his work of instilling evil into the minds of the angels, and he made it appear that he was seeking the good of the universe. As the anointed cherub, Lucifer had been highly exalted; he was greatly loved by the heavenly beings, and his influence over them was strong. Many of them listened to his suggestions and believed his words. "And there was war in heaven: Michael and his angels fought against the dragon; and the dragon fought and his angels, and prevailed not; neither was their place found any more in heaven." *S.D.A. Bible Commentary*, Vol. 7, 973.

But even as a sinner, man was in a different position from that of Satan. Lucifer in heaven had sinned in the light of God's glory. To him as to no other created being was given a revelation of God's love. Understanding the character of God, knowing His goodness, Satan chose to follow his own selfish, independent will. This choice was final. There was no more that God could do to save him. But man was deceived; his mind was darkened by Satan's sophistry. The height and depth of the love of God he did not know. For him there was hope in a knowledge of God's love. By beholding His character he might be drawn back to God. *Desire of Ages*, 761, 762.

21

Even when it was decided that he could no longer remain in heaven, Infinite Wisdom did not destroy Satan. Since the service of love can alone be acceptable to God, the allegiance of His creatures must rest upon a conviction of His justice and benevolence. The inhabitants of heaven and of other worlds, being unprepared to comprehend the nature or consequences of sin, could not then have seen the justice and mercy of God in the destruction of Satan. Had he been immediately blotted from existence, they would have served God from fear rather than from love. The influence of the deceiver would not have been fully destroyed, nor would the spirit of rebellion have been utterly eradicated. Evil must be permitted to come to maturity. For the good of the entire universe through ceaseless ages Satan must more fully develop his principles, that his charges against the divine government might be seen in their true light by all created beings, that the justice and mercy of God and the immutability of His law might forever be placed beyond all question.

Satan's rebellion was to be a lesson to the universe through all coming ages, a perpetual testimony to the nature and terrible results of sin. The working out of Satan's rule, its effects upon both men and angels, would show what must be the fruit of setting aside the divine authority. It would testify that with the existence of God's government and His law is bound up the well-being of all the creatures He has made. Thus the history of this terrible experiment of rebellion was to be perpetual safeguard to all holy intelligences, to prevent them from being deceived as to the nature of transgression, to save them from committing sin and suffering its punishments.

To the very close of the controversy in heaven the great usurper continued to justify himself. When it was announced that with all his sympathizers he must be expelled from the abodes of bliss, then the rebel leader boldly avowed his contempt for the Creator's law. He reiterated his claim that angels needed no control, but should be left to follow their own will, which would ever guide them right. He denounced the divine statutes as a restriction of their liberty and declared that it was his purpose to secure the abolition of law; that, freed from this restraint, the hosts of heaven might enter upon a more exalted, more glorious state of existence.

With one accord, Satan and his host threw the blame of their rebellion wholly upon Christ, declaring that if they had not been reproved, they would never have rebelled. Thus stubborn and defiant in their disloyalty, seeking vainly to overthrow the government of God, yet blasphemously claiming to be themselves the innocent victims of oppressive power, the archrebel and all his sympathizers were at last banished from heaven…

In the banishment of Satan from heaven, God declared His justice and maintained the honor of His throne. But when man had sinned through yielding to the deceptions of this apostate spirit, God gave an evidence of His love by yielding up His only-begotten Son to die for the fallen race. In the atonement the character of God is revealed. The mighty argument of the cross demonstrates to the whole universe that the course of sin which Lucifer had chosen was in no wise chargeable upon the government of God. *The Great Controversy*, 498–501.

Chapter 6

THE SERPENT

In order to accomplish his work unperceived, Satan chose to employ as his medium the serpent—a disguise well adapted for his purpose of deception. The serpent was then one of the wisest and most beautiful creatures on the earth. It had wings, and while flying through the air presented an appearance of dazzling brightness, having the color and brilliancy of burnished gold. Resting in the rich-laden branches of the forbidden tree and regaling itself with the delicious fruit, it was an object to arrest the attention and delight the eye of the beholder. Thus in the garden of peace lurked the destroyer, watching for his prey. *Patriarchs and Prophets*, 53.

Eve wandered away from the side of her husband, and was gazing with mingled curiosity and admiration upon the fruit of the forbidden tree. Satan, in the form of a serpent, conversed with Eve. The serpent had not the power of speech, but Satan used him as a medium. It was Satan that spoke, not the serpent. Eve was deceived, and thought it was the serpent. This serpent was a very beautiful creature with wings; and while flying through the air his appearance was very bright, resembling the color of burnished gold. He did not go upon the ground, but went from place to place through the air, and ate fruit like man. *Spiritual Gifts*, Volume 3, 39.

Satan assumes the form of a serpent, and enters Eden. The serpent was a beautiful creature, with wings; and while flying through the air, his appearance was bright, resembling burnished gold. He did not go upon the ground, but went from place to place through the air, and ate fruit like man. Satan entered into the serpent, and took his position in the tree of knowledge, and commenced leisurely eating of the fruit.

Eve, unconsciously at first, separated from her husband in her employment. When she became aware of the fact, she felt that there might be danger; but again she thought herself secure, even if she did not remain close by the side of her husband. She had wisdom and strength to know if evil came, and to meet it. This the angels had cautioned her not to do. Eve found herself gazing with mingled curiosity and admiration upon the fruit of the forbidden tree. She saw it was very lovely, and was reasoning with herself why God had so decidedly prohibited their eating or touching it. Now was Satan's opportunity. He addressed her as though he was able to divine her thoughts: "Yea, hath God said, Ye shall not eat of every tree of the garden?" Thus, with soft and pleasant words, and with musical voice, he addressed the wondering Eve. She was startled to hear a serpent speak. He extolled her beauty and exceeding loveliness, which was not displeasing to Eve. But she was amazed, for she knew that to the serpent God had not given the power of speech.

Eve's curiosity was aroused. Instead of fleeing from the spot, she listened to hear a serpent talk. It did not occur to her mind that it might be that fallen foe, using the serpent as a medium. It was Satan that spoke, not the serpent. Eve was beguiled, flattered, infatuated. Had she met a commanding personage, possessing a form like the angels, and resembling them, she would have been upon her guard. But that strange voice should have driven her to her husband's side to inquire of him why another should thus freely address her. But she enters into a controversy with the serpent. She answers his question, "We may eat of the fruit of the trees of the garden. But of the fruit of the tree which is in the midst of the garden, God hath said, Ye shall not eat of it, neither shall ye touch it, lest ye die." The serpent answers, "Ye shall not surely die; for God doth know that in the day ye eat thereof, then your eyes shall be opened, and ye shall be as gods, knowing good and evil." *The Spirit of Prophecy*, Volume One, 35, 36.

Here the father of lies made his assertion in direct contradiction to the expressed word of God. Satan assured Eve that she was created immortal, and that there was no possibility of her dying. He told her that God knew that if they ate of the tree of knowledge their understanding would be enlightened, expanded, and ennobled, making them equal with himself. And the serpent answered Eve, that the command of God forbidding them to eat of the tree of knowledge was given them to keep them in a state of subordination, that they should not obtain knowledge, which was power. He assured her that the fruit of this tree was desirable above every other tree in the garden to make one wise and exalt them equal with God. He has, said the serpent, refused you the fruit of the tree which is of all the trees the most desirable for its delicious flavor and exhilarating influence. Eve thought the discourse of the serpent very wise. She viewed the prohibition of God unjust. She looked with longing desire upon the tree laden with fruit which appeared very delicious. The serpent was eating it with apparent delight. She longed for this fruit above all the fruit of every variety which God had given her a perfect right to use. *Second Advent Review and Sabbath Herald*, 2-24-74.

The doctrine of the natural immortality of the soul is one error with which the enemy is deceiving man. This error is well-nigh universal. But who told men that they would not die? Who told them that God has reserved a portion of his universe where the wicked are to suffer through the ceaseless ages of eternity, without a particle of hope?—It was the serpent. God said that sinners would die. Satan declares that they will not die. Many believe the oft-repeated lies of the serpent to be genuine truth. They echo his words when they assert that God has ordained that sin shall be immortalized in a place of torment. *Advent Review and Sabbath Herald*, 3-16-97.

Witchcraft and sorcery are practiced in this Christian age and Christian nation, even more boldly than by the old-time magicians. Satan is finding access to thousands of minds by presenting himself under the guise of departed friends. The Scriptures of truth declare that "the dead know not anything." Their thoughts, their love, their hatred, have perished. The dead do not hold communion with the living. But Satan—true to his early cunning, when in the form of a serpent he deceived the mother of our race—employs this device to gain control of the minds of men. *The Signs of the Times*, 5-18-82.

Had Satan revealed himself in his real character, he would have been repulsed at once, for Adam and Eve had been warned against this dangerous foe; but he worked in the dark, concealing his purpose, that he might more effectually accomplish his object. Employing as his medium the serpent, then a creature of fascinating appearance, he addressed himself to Eve: "Hath God said, Ye shall not eat of every tree of the garden?" Genesis 3:1. Had Eve refrained from entering into argument with the tempter, she would have been safe; but she ventured to parley with him and fell a victim to his wiles. It is thus that many are still overcome. They doubt and argue concerning the requirements of God; and instead of obeying the divine commands, they accept human theories, which but disguise the devices of Satan. *The Great Controversy*, 531, 532.

Our first parents chose to believe the words, as they thought, of a serpent; yet he had given them no tokens of his love. He had done nothing for their happiness and benefit; while God had given them everything that was good for food, and pleasant to the sight. Everywhere the eye might rest was abundance and beauty; yet Eve was deceived by the serpent, to think that there was something withheld which would make them wise, even as God. Instead of believing and confiding in God, she basely distrusted his goodness, and cherished the words of Satan. *The Spirit of Prophecy*, Volume One, 40, 41.

The Lord then passed sentence upon the serpent: "Because thou hast done this, thou art cursed above all cattle, and above every beast of the field; upon thy belly shalt thou go, and dust shalt thou eat all the days of thy life." Since it had been employed as Satan's medium, the serpent was to share the visitation of divine judgment. From the most beautiful and admired of the creatures of the field, it was to become the most groveling and detested of them all, feared and hated by both man and beast. The words next addressed to the serpent applied directly to Satan himself, pointing forward to his ultimate defeat and destruction: "I will put enmity between thee and the woman, and between thy seed and her seed; it shall bruise thy head, and thou shalt bruise his heel." *Patriarchs and Prophets*, 58.

The murder of Abel was the first example of the enmity that God had declared would exist between the serpent and the seed of the woman—between Satan and his subjects and Christ and His followers. Through man's sin, Satan had gained control of the human race, but Christ would enable them to cast off his yoke. Whenever, through faith in the Lamb of God, a soul renounces the service of sin, Satan's wrath is kindled. The holy life of Abel testified against Satan's claim that it is impossible for man to keep God's law. When Cain, moved by the spirit of the wicked one, saw that he could not control Abel, he was so enraged that he destroyed his life. And wherever there are any who will stand in vindication of the righteousness of the law of God, the same spirit will be manifested against them. It is the spirit that through all the ages has set up the stake and kindled the burning pile for the disciples of Christ. But the cruelties heaped upon the follower of Jesus are instigated by Satan and his hosts because they cannot force him to submit to their control. It is the rage of a vanquished foe. Every martyr of Jesus has died a conqueror. Says the prophet, "They overcame him ["that old serpent, called the devil, and Satan"] by the blood of the Lamb, and by the word of their testimony; and they loved not their lives unto the death." Revelation 12:11, 9. *Patriarchs and Prophets*, 77.

When our first parents transgressed the holy law of God, the Lord promised that the seed of the woman should bruise the serpent's head; the serpent was to bruise the heel of the seed of the woman. But he was to have no power to touch the head. Humanity was lost, and Christ appeared as the world's Redeemer, the seed to whom the promises were made. He died to redeem mankind. Those who believed in him excited the wrath of the evil one, for Satan claimed man as his property. Satan persecuted the people of God. He tortured them, and put them to death; but in dying they became conquerors. They revealed in this steadfast faith a mightier one than Satan. Satan could torture and kill the body, but he could not touch the life that was hid with Christ in God. He could incarcerate in prison walls, but he could not bind the spirit. Living faith connected the people of God with Him who only hath immortality. They could look beyond the gloom to the glory that was to be revealed at the appearing of Jesus. Paul suffered much. He was persecuted from city to city, in perils oft, in prison, in scourging, in bonds, in fastings, in wearinesses and painful watchings, but he looked beyond the sufferings of the present time to glory beyond, and said: "I reckon that the sufferings of this present time are not worthy to be compared with the glory which shall be revealed in us." This is what God would have his people do. He would have us reckon and consider the rich reward of the eternal world, that we may appreciate the privileges that are brought within our reach through the plan of salvation. *The Signs of the Times*, 11-18-89.

Satan has sown plentifully the seed of dangerous heresies, that will produce a harvest of corruption, and will be as tares among the wheat. He is filling the hearts and minds of men with fables, and causing them to turn away their ears from hearing the truth. The advocates of truth are regarded as enemies to Christianity, and yet, although Satan causes the world to regard the followers of Christ as foes to progress, yet whenever a soul takes a decided stand for truth, the head of the serpent is bruised by the seed of the woman, and the serpent can bruise but the heel of the seed. When nominal Christianity is declared wanting, and is found insufficient, and practical godliness is alone declared genuine religion, the enmity of Satan is aroused at once, but his anger is an evidence of his bruising. He is seeking to hold the people in the deception of a form of godliness without its power, to keep them satisfied with a profession of piety; when their hearts are carnal and at enmity with the law of Jehovah. When the advocates of truth reveal the efficiency of truth in their life and character, a blow is struck against the kingdom of Satan. *The Signs of the Times*, 7-11-95.

...."And I will put enmity between thee and the woman, and between thy seed and her seed: it shall bruise thy head, and thou shalt bruise his heel." This prophecy refers not only to the enmity between Christ and Satan, but also to the enmity that exists between the world and the followers of the world's Redeemer. Christ was the special One who should bruise the head of the serpent; but the prophecy also includes all those who shall overcome the enemy by the blood of the Lamb, and by the word of their testimony. In the words addressed to the serpent is a delineation of the great, unended conflict that has been waging in the world from the beginning of sin. The earth is the battle-field for the conflict, and the result of the conflict, while it brings temporal loss upon the followers of Christ, will bring eternal ruin upon Satan, evil angels, and evil men, who unite with the enemy in the controversy against Christ. *The Youth's Instructor*, 10-11-94.

When sin first entered the world, God had promised a deliverer. He had said to the serpent, "I will put enmity between thee and the woman, and between thy seed and her seed; it shall bruise thy head, and thou shalt bruise his heel." When Jesus came to the world, his own nation despised him, his friends denied him, his brethren did not believe on him. The unbelief with which he was met was indeed a bruising of his heel. Christ, the world's Redeemer, was buffeted with temptation, but it had been written of him, "He shall not fail, nor be discouraged, till he have set judgment in the earth." Through the very bruising of his heel by Satan, because of affliction, temptation, and sorrow, Christ was gaining the victory in behalf of the human family; for he triumphed over his enemy in not yielding to his temptation, and thus bruised the head of the serpent. He endured the contradiction of sinners against himself, and every pang of anguish he suffered, every temptation he resisted, as man's substitute and surety, was elevating the human family in the scale of moral worth, and was procuring for man deliverance from Satan's power and bondage. The character of Satan, through his efforts to overcome and destroy the Son of God, was developing before the universe, and was being made manifest in its true malignity before the unfallen worlds that had been created by Christ. Every time he stung the heel of Christ with his murderous fang, the serpent was making more sure his own discomfiture and ruin. *The Signs of the Times*, 3-26-94.

The Commander of heaven was assailed by the tempter. He had no clear, unobstructed passage through the world. He was not left free and without hindrance to win to his kingdom the souls of men by his gracious mercy and loving-kindness. From the time that he was a helpless babe in Bethlehem, when the agencies of hell sought to destroy him in his infancy through the jealousy of Herod, until he came to Calvary's cross, he was continually assailed by the evil one. In the councils of Satan it was determined that he must be overcome. No human being had come into the world and escaped the power of the deceiver. The whole forces of the confederacy of evil were set upon his track to engage in warfare against him, and if possible to prevail over him. The fiercest and most inveterate enmity was put between the seed of the woman and the serpent. The serpent himself made Christ the mark of every weapon of hell. Satan knew that he must either conquer or himself be conquered. Success or failure involved too much for him to leave the work with any one of his agents of evil. The prince of evil himself must personally conduct the warfare, since all other enterprises were inferior to this. He came in determined opposition against Christ from the very beginning of his work. "And the child grew, and waxed strong in spirit, filled with wisdom; and the grace of God was upon him...And Jesus increased in wisdom and stature, and in favor with God and man." *Advent Review and Sabbath Herald*, 10-29-95.

The Lord says, "I will put enmity between thee and the woman." The enmity does not exist as a natural fact. As soon as Adam sinned, he was in harmony with the first great apostate and at war with God; and if God had not interfered in man's behalf, Satan and man would have formed a confederacy against heaven, and would have carried on united opposition against the God of hosts. There is no natural enmity between evil angels and evil men; both are evil through transgression of the law of God, and evil will always league against good. Fallen men and fallen angels enter into a desperate companionship. The prophecy of enmity between the serpent and the seed of the woman, was the first intimation that Satan had that God would provide a way of salvation for the fallen race. Satan had made his calculation that he would induce men to ally themselves with him as he had induced angels; and by this desperate confederacy, he would not hesitate to war against heaven, and seek to dethrone the Lord of hosts. *The Youth's Instructor*, 0-11-94.

When the Lord Jesus visited our earth, he brought with him renovating energy. He put enmity between the seed of the woman and the serpent. But there is no enmity between fallen angels and fallen men. Both, through apostasy, are evil; and wherever there is evil, with no disposition to repent, it will always league with Satan against God. Fallen men and fallen angels unite in a desperate struggle to destroy God's great standard of righteousness. There was a bond of sympathy among the angels that Satan succeeded in drawing into rebellion, and he made them his allies in the effort to dethrone God and to abolish his law. Satan's work in our world to day is to destroy the moral image of God in man, by making void the divine law; and our enemies are inspired by his spirit. By casting aside God's great standard of character, he can deprave human nature, and win men and women to his standard; for, "Where no law is, there is no transgression." With what triumph, then, he watches the professedly Christian world, as they earnestly do the very work he is doing. *Advent Review and Sabbath Herald*, 1-26-97.

The message proclaimed by the angel flying in the midst of heaven is the everlasting gospel, the same gospel that was declared in Eden when God said to the serpent, "I will put enmity between thee and the woman, and between thy seed and her seed; it shall bruise thy head, and thou shalt bruise his heel" [Gen. 3:15]. Here was the first promise of a Saviour who would stand on the field of battle to contest the power of Satan and prevail against him. Christ came to our world to represent the character of God as it is represented in His holy law; for His law is a transcript of His character. Christ was both the law and the gospel. The angel that proclaims the everlasting gospel proclaims the law of God; for the gospel of salvation brings men to obedience of the law, whereby their characters are formed after the divine similitude. *Manuscript Releases*, Vol. Seventeen, 7, 8.

Satan has come down with great power, working with all deceivableness of unrighteousness in them that perish; but it is not necessary for any to be deceived; and we shall not be if we have fully taken our stand with Christ to follow him through evil as well as through good report. The serpent's head will soon be bruised and crushed. The glorious memorial of God's wonderful power is soon to be restored to its rightful place. Then paradise lost will be paradise restored. God's plan for the redemption of man will be complete. The Son of Man will bestow upon the righteous the crown of everlasting life, and they shall "serve him day and night in his temple; and he that sitteth on the throne shall dwell among them. They shall hunger no more, neither thirst any more; neither shall the sun light on them, nor any heat. For the Lamb which is in the midst of the throne shall feed them, and shall lead them unto living fountains of waters: and God shall wipe away all tears from their eyes." *Advent Review and Sabbath Herald*, 9-05-99.

Chapter 7

SATAN'S AGENDA

Christ came to represent the character of his Father, to win man back to his allegiance to God, to reconcile man to God. He proposed to meet the foe and unmask his arts, that man might be able to make choice of whom he would serve. Satan had been Lucifer, the light-bearer, the sharer of God's glory in heaven, and second to Jesus in power and majesty. In the words of inspiration he is described as the one who "sealest up the sum, full of wisdom, and perfect in beauty." But Lucifer had perverted the beauty and power with which he was endowed by the Creator, and his light had become darkness. When through his rebellion he was cast out of heaven, he determined to make man his victim, and the earth his kingdom. He cast the blame of his rebellion upon Christ, and in determined hatred of God, sought to wound Him through the fall of man. In the happiness and peace of Eden, he beheld a vision of the bliss that he had forever lost, and he determined to excite in the hearts of God's creatures the same bitterness that he himself felt, so that their songs of praise and thanksgiving might be turned to reproach against their Maker. *Bible Echo and Signs of the Times*, 11-01-92

The holy inhabitants of other worlds were watching with the deepest interest the events taking place on the earth. In the condition of the world that existed before the Flood they saw illustrated the results of the administration which Lucifer had endeavored to establish in heaven, in rejecting the authority of Christ and casting aside the law of God. In those high-handed sinners of the antediluvian world they saw the subjects over whom Satan held sway. The thoughts of men's hearts were only evil continually. Genesis 6:5. Every emotion, every impulse and imagination, was at war with the divine principles of purity and peace and love. It was an example of the awful depravity resulting from Satan's policy to remove from God's creatures the restraint of His holy law. *Patriarchs and Prophets*, 78, 79.

In the rebellion of Korah is seen the working out, upon a narrower stage, of the same spirit that led to the rebellion of Satan in heaven. It was pride and ambition that prompted Lucifer to complain of the government of God, and to seek the overthrow of the order which had been established in heaven. Since his fall it has been his object to infuse the same spirit of envy and discontent, the same ambition for position and honor, into the minds of men. He thus worked upon the minds of Korah, Dathan, and Abiram, to arouse the desire for self-exaltation and excite envy, distrust, and rebellion. Satan caused them to reject God as their leader, by rejecting the men of God's appointment. Yet while in their murmuring against Moses and Aaron they blasphemed God, they were so deluded as to think themselves righteous, and to regard those who had faithfully reproved their sins as actuated by Satan. *Patriarchs and Prophets*, 403.

There is a grand rebellion in the earthly universe. Is there not a great leader of that rebellion? Is not Satan the life and soul of every species of rebellion which he himself has instigated? Is he not the first great apostate from God? A rebellion exists. Lucifer revolted from his allegiance and makes war on the divine government. Christ is appointed to put down the rebellion. He makes this world His battlefield. He stands at the head of the human family. He clothes His divinity with humanity and He passes over the ground where Adam fell and endures all the assaults of Satan's temptations, but He does not yield in a single instance. *S.D.A. Bible Commentary*, Vol. 4, 1163.

From the beginning, it has been the special doctrine of the adversary of God and man, that the law of God was faulty and objectionable. He has ever represented the royal law of liberty, as oppressive and unendurable. He has denoted it "a yoke of bondage." He has declared that it was impossible for man to keep the precepts of Jehovah. This has been, and still is, the work of Satan. This is the seductive doctrine that devils are seeking to spread throughout the world. "No law" is the cry of the enemy of God. Shall we go over to the side of the great rebel? If we do, it will be our ruin. Shall we make void the law of God, because Satan tells us that we should be more free, and happier, if we would do so? Were Adam and Eve happier, and did they walk in more liberty, when they received and acted upon these suggestions of the evil one? *Advent Review and Sabbath Herald*, 7-31-88.

Lucifer took the position that as a result of the law of God, wrong existed in heaven and on this earth. This brought against God's government the charge of being arbitrary. But this is a falsehood, framed by the author of all falsehoods. God's government is a government of free-will, and there is no act of rebellion or obedience which is not an act of free-will. *The Signs of the Times*, 6-05-01

In heaven itself this law was broken. Sin originated in self-seeking. Lucifer, the covering cherub, desired to be first in heaven. He sought to gain control of heavenly beings, to draw them away from their Creator, and to win their homage to himself. Therefore he misrepresented God, attributing to Him the desire for self-exaltation. With his own evil characteristics he sought to invest the loving Creator. Thus he deceived angels. Thus he deceived men. He led them to doubt the word of God, and to distrust His goodness. Because God is a God of justice and terrible majesty, Satan caused them to look upon Him as severe and unforgiving. Thus he drew men to join him in rebellion against God, and the night of woe settled down upon the world. *The Desire of Ages*, 21, 22.

Lucifer in heaven desired to be first in power and authority; he wanted to be God, to have the rulership of heaven; and to this end he won many of the angels to his side. When with his rebel host he was cast out from the courts of God, the work of rebellion and self-seeking was continued on earth. Through the temptation to self-indulgence and ambition Satan accomplished the fall of our first parents; and from that time to the present the gratification of human ambition and the indulgence of selfish hopes and desires have proved the ruin of mankind. *Counsels to Parents, Teachers, and Students, 32, 33.*

God is love. The evil that is in the world comes not from His hands, but from our great adversary, whose work it has ever been to deprave man, and enfeeble and pervert his faculties. But God has not left us in the ruin wrought by the fall. Every faculty has been placed in reach by our Heavenly Father, that men may, through well-directed efforts, regain their first perfection, and stand complete in Christ. In this work God expects us to do our part. We are His – His purchased possession. The human family cost God and His Son Jesus Christ an infinite price. *Fundamentals of Christian Education, 429.*

In the prophecy of Zechariah is brought to view Satan's accusing work, and the work of Christ in resisting the adversary of His people. The prophet says, "He showed me Joshua the high priest standing before the angel of the Lord, and Satan standing at his right hand to resist him. And the Lord said unto Satan, The Lord rebuke thee, O Satan; even the Lord that hath chosen Jerusalem rebuke thee: is not this a brand plucked out of the fire? Now Joshua was clothed with filthy garments, and stood before the angel." Zech. 3:1–3.

The people of God are here represented as a criminal on trial. Joshua, as high priest, is seeking for a blessing for his people, who are in great affliction. While he is pleading before God, Satan is standing at his right hand as his adversary. He is accusing the children of God, and making their case appear as desperate as possible. He presents before the Lord their evil doings and their defects. He shows their faults and failures, hoping they will appear of such a character in the eyes of Christ that He will render them no help in their great need. Joshua, as the representative of God's people, stands under condemnation, clothed with filthy garments. Aware of the sins of his people, he is weighed down with discouragement. Satan is pressing upon his soul a sense of guiltiness that makes him feel almost hopeless. Yet there he stands as a suppliant, with Satan arrayed against him. *Christ's Object Lessons*, 166, 167.

"Let no Christian be found an accuser of the brethren. Satan is the one who bears this title; he accuses them before God day and night, he stirs up the enemies of our faith to accuse us, and he prompts those of like precious faith to criticize and condemn one another. We are not to take part in his work. These are days of trial and of great peril; the adversary of souls is upon the track of every one; and while we stand out separate from the world, we should press together in faith and love. United, we are strong; divided, we are weak....*Advent Review and Sabbath Herald*, 12-06-06.

On the other side are Satan and his angels, with all his agents on earth, who make every effort and use every device to advance error and wrong, and to cover up their hideousness and deformity with a pleasing garb. Selfishness, hypocrisy, and every species of deception, Satan clothes with a garment of apparent truth and righteousness, and triumphs in his success, even with ministers and people who profess to understand his wiles. The greater distance they keep from Christ their great Leader, the less they are like Him in character, the more close is their resemblance in life and character to the servants of their great adversary, and the more sure is he of them at last. While they profess to be servants of Christ, they are servants of sin. Some ministers have their minds too much on the wages they receive. They labor for wages and lose sight of the sacredness and importance of the work. *Testimonies for the Church*, Vol. One, 467.

The great controversy between Christ and Satan, that has been carried on for almost six thousand years, is soon to close. And yet how few have their attention called to this matter, how few realize that we are living amid the closing scenes of earth's history! Satan is working diligently, binding his sheaves preparatory to gathering in his harvest. He is uniting the elements of his kingdom for the final struggle. Since his fall, he has been the great adversary of God and man, and has shown a masterly activity in trying to defeat our Saviour's efforts in our behalf. He thinks that because so many readily yield to his temptations and believe his lies, he may yet gain some advantage over Christ, who left the royal courts of Heaven that he might defeat this wily foe on his own battle-field, and open a way whereby man might escape from his cruel power.

He is called in the Bible, Satan, Beelzebub, the serpent, the deceiver, a liar, the accuser of the brethren, the prince of the power of the air, the prince of darkness, and the god of this world. Frightful names, infernal agencies! This fallen spirit, so malignant and subtle, is walking about like a roaring lion, seeking whom he may devour. When there is no special effort made to resist his power, when profound indifference prevails in the church and in the world, he is not concerned; for he is in no danger of losing those whom he is leading captive at his will. But when the attention is called to eternal things, and souls are inquiring, "What shall I do to be saved?" he is on the ground, seeking to match his power against the power of Christ, and doubling his efforts to counteract the influences of the Holy Spirit. Angels of God, with Jesus at their head, are present to press back the powers of darkness; but no one is forced to accept Jesus, and no one can be compelled by Satan's power to reject him. *The Signs of the Times*, 5-08-84.

Although the law of God is of a holy and unchangeable character, the adversary of God and man, the first great rebel who transgressed its precepts in Heaven, has led men in all ages to war against God. Through all manner of deceptions he has gathered them under the black banner of rebellion. But Jesus came to our world to bring to men moral power to resist the devices of Satan, and to become loyal subjects to the God of Heaven. As the sinner sees that sin is the transgression of the law, and that the law is the foundation of God's government in Heaven and in earth, he makes haste to place his feet in the path of righteousness, that he may be without offense till the day of Christ. *The Signs of the Times*, 7-06-88.

Chapter 8

SATAN'S HOSTS

Evil spirits, in the beginning created sinless, were equal in nature, power, and glory with the holy beings that are now God's messengers. But fallen through sin, they are leagued together for the dishonor of God and the destruction of men. United with Satan in his rebellion, and with him cast out from heaven, they have, through all succeeding ages, co-operated with him in his warfare against the divine authority. We are told in Scripture of their confederacy and government, of their various orders, of their intelligence and subtlety, and of their malicious designs against the peace and happiness of men.

Old Testament history presents occasional mention of their existence and agency; but it was during the time when Christ was upon the earth that evil spirits manifested their power in the most striking manner. Christ had come to enter upon the plan devised for man's redemption, and Satan determined to assert his right to control the world. He had succeeded in establishing idolatry in every part of the earth except the land of Palestine. To the only land that had not fully yielded to the tempter's sway, Christ came to shed upon the people the light of heaven. Here two rival powers claimed supremacy. Jesus was stretching out His arms of love, inviting all who would to find pardon and peace in Him. The hosts of darkness saw that they did not possess unlimited control, and they understood that if Christ's mission should be successful, their rule was soon to end. Satan raged like a chained lion and defiantly exhibited his power over the bodies as well as the souls of men. *The Great Controversy*, 513, 514.

Let all heed the warning, "Remember therefore how thou hast received, and heard, and hold fast, and repent. If therefore thou shalt not watch, I will come on thee as a thief, and thou shalt not know what hour I will come upon thee" (Revelation 3:3). Satan is using all his science in playing the game of life for human souls. His angels are mingling with men and instructing them in the mysteries of evil. These fallen angels will draw away disciples after them, will talk with men, and will set forth principles that are as false as can be, leading souls into paths of deception. These angels are to be found all over the world, presenting the wonderful things that will soon appear in a more decided light. God calls upon His people to gain an understanding of the mystery of godliness. Jesus Christ is our dependence, and the Lord calls upon His people to beware of following a course that would rob them of their usefulness. *Manuscript Release No. 760: The Integrity of the Sanctuary Truth*, 17.

Genuine faith works by love, and purifies the soul. There is a faith that has power to cleanse the life from sin. The devils believe that Christ came into this world as man's Redeemer, that he wrought mighty miracles, that he was one with the Father, that he died a shameful death to save fallen man. The devils believe that he rose from the dead, that he ascended into the heavens, and sitteth on the right hand of the Father. The devils believe that he is coming again, and that shortly, with power and great glory, taking vengeance on them that know not God and obey not the gospel. They believe all that is recorded in the Old and New Testaments. But will this faith save the demons of darkness? They have not the faith that works by love and purifies the soul. That faith, and that alone, which cleanses the soul-temple, is the genuine faith. Everything that defileth must be put away, all filthiness of the flesh and spirit must be removed from us, if we would enter in through the gates into the city. Jesus says, "If ye love me, keep my commandments." *The Signs of the Times*, 2-17-90.

The work before the servants of God is to present Jesus. The work for the ministers of Christ is to hang their helpless souls upon His merit. Men who turn away from the path of obedience and make transgression of the law of God a virtue are under the inspiration of the archdeceiver. They are blinded by his power. They need to have before them a representation of what the truth can do in enabling men to preserve a Christlike temper when tempted to become imperious and impatient. The enemies of the truth want to provoke those who teach the binding claims of the law of God. If there is retaliation on our part, Satan's hosts triumph. He has found a weak place in the armor. By their mean course of action the agents of Satan try to tempt the advocates of truth to say and do things that will not be commendable. *Testimonies to Ministers and Gospel Workers*, 247, 248.

Christ is the ladder that Jacob saw, on which descended and ascended the angels of God, while the glory of God illuminated every round of the ladder from the highest heaven to the earth. Christ spanned the gulf that separated man from God, and earth from heaven, and he is working continually in our behalf, and individually we are to co-operate with him and with the heavenly intelligences. But Christ can do nothing for us without our co-operation, and we can do nothing without him. Satan and his angels are at war with us, and they will be at war with us to the end of the world, and Jesus has told us, "Without me ye can do nothing." This is the lesson that Christ has been teaching his children through all ages, and in every generation. *Advent Review and Sabbath Herald*, 7-19-92.

The fact that men have been possessed with demons, is clearly stated in the New Testament. The persons thus afflicted were not merely suffering with disease from natural causes. Christ had perfect understanding of that with which He was dealing, and He recognized the direct presence and agency of evil spirits.

A striking example of their number, power, and malignity, and also of the power and mercy of Christ, is given in the Scripture account of the healing of the demoniacs at Gadara. Those wretched maniacs, spurning all restraint, writhing, foaming, raging, were filling the air with their cries, doing violence to themselves, and endangering all who should approach them. Their bleeding and disfigured bodies and distracted minds presented a spectacle well pleasing to the prince of darkness. One of the demons controlling the sufferers declared: "My name is Legion: for we are many." Mark 5:9. In the Roman army a legion consisted of from three to five thousand men. Satan's hosts also are marshaled in companies, and the single company to which these demons belonged numbered no less than a legion. *The Great Controversy*, 514.

With authority He bids the unclean spirits come out of them. The unfortunate men realize that One is near who can save them from the tormenting demons. They fall at the Saviour's feet to entreat His mercy; but when their lips are opened, the demons speak through them, crying, "What have we to do with Thee, Jesus, Thou Son of God? art Thou come hither to torment us?" Matthew 8:29. *The Ministry of Healing*, 96.

Satan's armies are many, and God's people must spread over all the world, planting the standard of truth in the dark places of the earth and doing their utmost to destroy Satan's kingdom. *Evangelism*, 18.

We need in all our churches the evidences of the meekness of Christ. In order to do intelligently the solemn work committed to us, we must hide self in Jesus Christ. We have a short time in which to accomplish the work that is essential. Let us earnestly prepare for the conflict that is before us, for Satan's armies are marshalling for the last great struggle. I am instructed to say to all our people, Let your light so shine in words and deeds, that you will reveal that truth is cherished in the heart. *Manuscript Releases*, Volume Nineteen, 376.

The deception of sin had reached its height. All the agencies for depraving the souls of men had been put in operation. The Son of God, looking upon the world, beheld suffering and misery. With pity He saw how men had become victims of satanic cruelty. He looked with compassion upon those who were being corrupted, murdered, and lost. They had chosen a ruler who chained them to his car as captives. Bewildered and deceived, they were moving on in gloomy procession toward eternal ruin,—to death in which is no hope of life, toward night to which comes no morning. Satanic agencies were incorporated with men. The bodies of human beings, made for the dwelling place of God, had become the habitation of demons. The senses, the nerves, the passions, the organs of men, were worked by supernatural agencies in the indulgence of the vilest lust. The very stamp of demons was impressed upon the countenances of men. Human faces reflected the expression of the legions of evil with which they were possessed. Such was the prospect upon which the world's Redeemer looked. What a spectacle for Infinite Purity to behold! *The Desire of Ages*, 36.

Those possessed with devils are usually represented as being in a condition of great suffering; yet there were exceptions to this rule. For the sake of obtaining supernatural power, some welcomed the satanic influence. These of course had no conflict with the demons. Of this class were those who possessed the spirit of divination,—Simon Magus, Elymas the sorcerer, and the damsel who followed Paul and Silas at Philippi. *The Great Controversy*, 516.

…"What shall I do then with Jesus which is called Christ?" Pilate asked. Again the surging multitude roared like demons. Demons themselves, in human form, were in the crowd, and what could be expected but the answer, "Let Him be crucified"? *The Desire of Ages*, 733.

Fearful sights of a supernatural character will soon be revealed in the heavens, in token of the power of miracle-working demons. The spirits of devils will go forth to the kings of the earth and to the whole world, to fasten them in deception, and urge them on to unite with Satan in his last struggle against the government of heaven. By these agencies, rulers and subjects will be alike deceived. Persons will arise pretending to be Christ Himself, and claiming the title and worship which belong to the world's Redeemer. They will perform wonderful miracles of healing and will profess to have revelations from heaven contradicting the testimony of the Scriptures. *The Great Controversy*, 624.

The great power that attends Spiritualism has its origin in the great leading rebel, Satan, the prince of devils. It is through his artifice that evil angels have been able to substitute themselves for the dead, and through lying hypocrisy they have led men to have intercourse with devils. Those who commune with the supposed spirits of the dead are communing with those who will have a corrupting, demoralizing power upon the mind. Christ commanded that we should have no intercourse with sorcerers and with those who have familiar spirits. This class are represented in the Gospel as among those who shall perish in their iniquity, — "the fearful, and unbelieving, and the abominable, and murderers, and whoremongers, and sorcerers, and idolaters, and all liars, shall have their part in the lake which burneth with fire and brimstone." *The Signs of the Times*, 5-28-94.

I saw that the saints must get a thorough understanding of present truth, which they will be obliged to maintain from the Scriptures. They must understand the state of the dead; for the spirits of devils will yet appear to them, professing to be beloved friends and relatives, who will declare to them that the Sabbath has been changed, also other unscriptural doctrines. They will do all in their power to excite sympathy and will work miracles before them to confirm what they declare. The people of God must be prepared to withstand these spirits with the Bible truth that the dead know not anything, and that they who appear to them are the spirits of devils. Our minds must not be taken up with things around us, but must be occupied with the present truth and a preparation to give a reason of our hope with meekness and fear. We must seek wisdom from on high that we may stand in this day of error and delusion. *Early Writings*, 87, 88.

Could human beings know the number of the evil angels, could they know their devices and their activity, there would be far less pride and frivolity. Satan is the prince of demons. The evil angels over whom he rules do his bidding. Through them he multiplies his agencies throughout the world. He instigates all the evil that exists in our world. *S.D.A. Bible Commentary*, Vol. Six, 1119.

Satan was exulting that he had succeeded in debasing the image of God in humanity. Then Jesus came to restore in man the image of his Maker. None but Christ can fashion anew the character that has been ruined by sin. He came to expel the demons that had controlled the will. He came to lift us up from the dust, to reshape the marred character after the pattern of His divine character, and to make it beautiful with His own glory. *The Desire of Ages*, 37.

Chapter 9

SATAN'S METHODS

It is a masterpiece of Satan's deceptions to keep the minds of men searching and conjecturing in regard to that which God has not made known and which He does not intend that we shall understand. It was thus that Lucifer lost his place in heaven. He became dissatisfied because all the secrets of God's purposes were not confided to him, and he entirely disregarded that which was revealed concerning his own work in the lofty position assigned him. By arousing the same discontent in the angels under his command, he caused their fall. Now he seeks to imbue the minds of men with the same spirit and to lead them also to disregard the direct commands of God. *The Great Controversy*, 523.

The glory and peace of heaven, and the joy of communion with God, were but dimly comprehended by men; but they were well known to Lucifer, the covering cherub. Since he had lost heaven, he was determined to find revenge by causing others to share his fall. This he would do by causing them to undervalue heavenly things, and to set the heart upon things of earth. *Desire of Ages*, 115, 116.

The greatness and power with which the Creator endowed Lucifer he has perverted; and yet, when it suits his purpose, he can impart to men sentiments that are enchanting. Everything in nature comes from God; yet Satan can inspire his agents with thoughts that appear elevating and noble. Did he not come to Christ with quotations of Scripture when he designed to overthrow Him with his specious temptations? This is the way in which he comes to man, as an angel of light disguising his temptations under an appearance of goodness, and making men believe him to be the friend rather than the enemy of humanity. It is in this way that he has deceived and seduced the race,—beguiling them with subtle temptations, bewildering them with specious deceptions. *Fundamentals of Christian Education,* 176.

Here, for a time, Satan had the advantage; and he exulted in his arrogated superiority, in this one respect, to the angels of Heaven, and even to God himself. While Satan can employ fraud and sophistry to accomplish his objects, God cannot lie; while Lucifer, like the serpent, can choose a tortuous course, turning, twisting, gliding, to conceal himself, God moves only in a direct, straight-forward line. Satan had disguised himself in a cloak of falsehood, and for a time it was impossible to tear off the covering, so that the hideous deformity of his character could be seen. He must be left to reveal himself in his cruel, artful, wicked works. *The Spirit of Prophecy,* Volume Four, 319.

Cast out of heaven, Satan set up his kingdom in this world, and ever since, he has been untiringly striving to seduce human beings from their allegiance to God. He uses the same power that he used in heaven—the influence of mind on mind. Men become tempters of their fellow men. The strong, corrupting sentiments of Satan are cherished, and they exert a masterly, compelling power. Under the influence of these sentiments, men bind up with one another in confederacies (Letter 114, 1903). *S.D.A. Bible Commentary,* Vol. Seven, 973.

While Satan is constantly seeking to blind their minds to the fact, let Christians never forget that they "wrestle not against flesh and blood, but against principalities, against powers, against the rulers of the darkness of this world, against wicked spirits in high places." Ephesians 6:12, margin. The inspired warning is sounding down the centuries to our time: "Be sober, be vigilant; because your adversary the devil, as a roaring lion, walketh about, seeking whom he may devour." 1 Peter 5:8. "Put on the whole armor of God, that ye may be able to stand against the wiles of the devil." Ephesians 6:11. *The Great Controversy,* 510.

Two nights ago I never slept a wink. I lay awake for hours praying. The world is going to be surprised by the Lord's coming. Your work here will convince others that we are in earnest. Take hold here with all your heart. Let no evil work go from your hands. The world is going mad, stirred up by Lucifer, who is working upon the minds of men. *Pacific Union Recorder*, 1-12-11.

Our chief adversary is the devil. He is represented as going about as a roaring lion, seeking whom he may devour. When he finds men and women who have become self-exalted, as he himself became in heaven, and full of jealousy, and ambitious for power and prominence, he knows just how to lead them by his temptations so that they will prostitute their powers to his use, and become his agents in ruining their fellow-men. He is ready to work through his human agents in such a way as to conceal himself from view, in order that he may set in operation a train of circumstances that will lead men away from God, lead them away from the association and companionship of those who are connected with Christ, and influence them to do the work of annoying, distressing, and discouraging those who love Jesus. The spell of temptation holds these souls like a bewitching charm. "Every man is tempted, when he is drawn away of his own lust, and enticed." Yielding to the voice of the tempter, the tempted one surrenders virtue and principle, and in place of turning at once to God with contrition and repentance, he severs the last link whereby God's power can work for him, and hell triumphs because he has become the prey of the enemy. When the adversary thus bewitches the soul and entraps the unwary feet, he then represents God as inexorable and unforgiving, declaring that it will be of no use to make a confession of sin now, for God will not pardon. Let not the tempted soul listen to the voice of the accuser and destroyer, and take the way of the hopeless apostate, and plunge into midnight darkness. Remember the promise of God. He says, "Return unto the Lord thy God; for thou hast fallen by thine iniquity. Take with you words, and turn to the Lord; say unto him, Take away all iniquity, and receive us graciously." The Lord answers, "I will heal their backsliding, I will love them freely; for mine anger is turned away from him." Break with the enemy, and seek the presence of Jesus; with tears of confession and with penitential grief urge once more your suit at the throne of grace. The Lord will hear, the Lord will answer; return ere it be too late. *Advent Review and Sabbath Herald*, 12-11-94.

The body is the only medium through which the mind and the soul are developed for the upbuilding of character. Hence it is that the adversary of souls directs his temptations to the enfeebling and degrading of the physical powers. His success here means the surrender to evil of the whole being. The tendencies of our physical nature, unless under the dominion of a higher power, will surely work ruin and death. *Counsels on Diet and Foods*, 73.

The adversary of souls is working in these last days with greater power than ever before to accomplish the ruin of man through the indulgence of appetite and passions. And many who are held by Satan under the power of slavish appetite are the professed followers of Christ. They profess to worship God, while appetite is their god. Their unnatural desires for these indulgences are not controlled by reason or judgment. Those who are slaves to tobacco will see their families suffering for the conveniences of life, and for necessary food, yet they have not the power of will to forego their tobacco. The clamors of appetite prevail over natural affection. Appetite, which they have in common with the brute, controls them. The cause of Christianity, and even humanity, would not in any case be met, if dependent upon those in the habitual use of tobacco and liquor. If they had means to use only in one direction, the treasury of God would not be replenished, but they would have their tobacco and liquor. The tobacco idolater will not deny his appetite for the cause of God. *Second Advent Review and Sabbath Herald*, 9-08-74.

It was the adversary of all good who instigated the invention of the ever-changing fashions. He desires nothing so much as to bring grief and dishonor to God by working the misery and ruin of human beings. One of the means by which he most effectually accomplishes this is the devices of fashion, that weaken the body, as well as enfeeble the mind and belittle the soul. *Counsels on Health*, 91.

The only safety for the young is in unceasing watchfulness and humble prayer. They need not flatter themselves that they can be Christians without these. Satan conceals his temptations and his devices under a cover of light, as when he approached Christ in the wilderness. He was then in appearance as one of the heavenly angels. The adversary of our souls will approach us as a heavenly guest, and the apostle recommends sobriety and vigilance as our only safety. The young who indulge in carelessness and levity, and who neglect Christian duties, are continually falling under the temptations of the enemy, instead of overcoming as Christ overcame. *Testimonies for the Church*, Volume Three, 374.

Our great adversary is constantly working with power to allure the youth to self-indulgence, pride, and extravagance, that their minds and hearts may be so fully taken up with these things that there will be no place for God in their affections. He is by these means warping the character and dwarfing the intellect of the youth of this generation. It is the duty of parents to counteract his working. Every influence brought to bear upon the young people to preserve in their hearts true, unaffected humility, and the knowledge of the divine will, will aid in holding them back from being corrupted with the vices of this age. *Counsels on Sabbath School Work*, 139.

The young generally conduct themselves as though the precious hours of probation, while mercy lingers, were one grand holiday, and they were placed in this world merely for their own amusement, to be gratified with a continued round of excitement. Satan has been making special efforts to lead them to find happiness in worldly amusements and to justify themselves by endeavoring to show that these amusements are harmless, innocent, and even important for health. *Testimonies for the Church*, Volume One, 501.

The great adversary of souls is seeking to bring a dead, lifeless spiritual atmosphere into all our institutions. He works to turn and twist every circumstance to his own advantage, to the exclusion of Jesus Christ. Today, as in the days of Christ, God cannot do many mighty works because of the unbelief of those who stand in responsible positions. The converting power of God is needed before they will understand the word of God, and be willing to humble themselves before Him as learners. *Counsels to Parents, Teachers, and Students*, 373, 374.

He has power to bring before men the appearance of their departed friends. The counterfeit is perfect; the familiar look, the words, the tone, are reproduced with marvelous distinctness. Many are comforted with the assurance that their loved ones are enjoying the bliss of heaven, and without suspicion of danger, they give ear "to seducing spirits, and doctrines of devils." *The Great Controversy*, 552.

Many will be confronted by the spirits of devils personating beloved relatives or friends and declaring the most dangerous heresies. These visitants will appeal to our tenderest sympathies and will work miracles to sustain their pretensions. We must be prepared to withstand them with the Bible truth that the dead know not anything and that they who thus appear are the spirits of devils. *The Great Controversy*, 560.

Had the minister utterly refused to listen to the colored, one-sided statements of any, had he given words of advice in accordance with the Bible rule and said, like Nehemiah, "I am doing a great work, so that I cannot come down," that church would have been in a far better condition. This work of withdrawing men from their fields of labor has been repeated again and again in the progress of this cause. It is the device of the great adversary of souls to hinder the work of

God. When souls that are upon the point of deciding in favor of the truth are thus left to unfavorable influences, they lose their interest, and it is very rarely that so powerful an impression can again be made upon them. Satan is ever seeking some device to call the minister from his field of labor at this critical point, that the results of his labors may be lost. *Evangelism*, 691.

Ministers of the gospel, God's messengers to their fellowmen, should never lose sight of their mission and their responsibilities. If they lose their connection with heaven, they are in greater danger than others, and can exert a stronger influence for wrong. Satan watches them continually, waiting for some weakness to develop, through which he may make a successful attack upon them. And how he triumphs when he succeeds! for an ambassador for Christ, off his guard, allows the great adversary to secure many souls to himself. *Gospel Workers* (1915), 17.

I have been and still am instructed regarding the necessities required for the work in the cities. We must quietly secure buildings, without defining all we intend to do. We must use great wisdom in what we say, lest our way be hedged up. Lucifer is an ingenious worker, drawing from our people all possible knowledge, that he may, if possible, defeat the plans laid to arouse our cities. On some points silence is eloquence. *Evangelism*, 75.

As Lucifer sees that we are making efforts to work the cities as if we meant to give the last message, his wrath will be aroused, and he will employ every device in his power to hinder the work.... *Manuscript Releases*, Volume Five, 169.

Satan therefore laid his plans to war more successfully against the government of God by planting his banner in the Christian church. If the followers of Christ could be deceived and led to displease God, then their strength, fortitude, and firmness would fail, and they would fall an easy prey.

The great adversary now endeavored to gain by artifice what he had failed to secure by force. Persecution ceased, and in its stead were substituted the dangerous allurements of temporal prosperity and worldly honor. Idolaters were led to receive a part of the Christian faith, while they rejected other essential truths. They professed to accept Jesus as the Son of God and to believe in His death and resurrection, but they had no conviction of sin and felt no need of repentance or of a change of heart. With some concessions on their part they proposed that Christians should make concessions, that all might unite on the platform of belief in Christ. *The Great Controversy*, 42.

Satan well knew that the Holy Scriptures would enable men to discern his deceptions and withstand his power. It was by the word that even the Saviour of the world had resisted his attacks. At every assault, Christ presented the shield of eternal truth, saying, "It is written." To every suggestion of the adversary, He opposed the wisdom and power of the word. In order for Satan to maintain his sway over men, and establish the authority of the papal usurper, he must keep them in ignorance of the Scriptures. The Bible would exalt God and place finite men in their true position; therefore its sacred truths must be concealed and suppressed. This logic was adopted by the Roman Church. For hundreds of years the circulation of the Bible was prohibited. The people were forbidden to read it or to have it in their houses, and unprincipled priests and prelates interpreted its teachings to sustain their pretensions. Thus the pope came to be almost universally acknowledged as the vicegerent of God on earth, endowed with authority over church and state. *The Great Controversy*, 51.

The darkness of the evil one encloses those who neglect to pray. The whispered temptations of the enemy entice them to sin; and it is all because they do not make use of the privileges that God has given them in the divine appointment of prayer. Why should the sons and daughters of God be reluctant to pray, when prayer is the key in the hand of faith to unlock heaven's storehouse, where are treasured the boundless resources of Omnipotence? Without unceasing prayer and diligent watching, we are in danger of growing careless, and of deviating from the right path. The adversary seeks continually to obstruct the way to the mercy-seat, that we may not be earnest supplication and faith obtain grace and power to resist temptation. *Advent Review and Sabbath Herald*, 12-08-04.

By the cry, Liberality, men are blinded to the devices of their adversary, while he is all the time working steadily for the accomplishment of his object. As he succeeds in supplanting the Bible by human speculations, the law of God is set aside, and the churches are under the bondage of sin while they claim to be free. *The Great Controversy*, 522.

I have been shown that we must be guarded on every side, and perseveringly resist the insinuations and devices of Satan. He has transformed himself into an angel of light, and is deceiving and leading thousands captive. The advantages he takes of the science of the human mind, is tremendous. Here, serpent-like, he imperceptibly creeps in to corrupt the work of God. The miracles and works of Christ, he makes all human. If Satan should make an open, bold attack upon Christianity, it would bring the Christian in distress and agony at the feet of his Redeemer, and the strong and mighty Deliverer would affright the bold adversary away. But Satan, transformed into an angel of light, works upon the mind to allure from the only safe and right path. The sciences of phrenology, psychology, and mesmerism, have been the channel through which Satan has come more directly to this generation, and wrought with that power which was to characterize his work near the close of probation. *Spiritual Gifts*, Volume 4B, 80.

Satan leads many to believe that God will overlook their unfaithfulness in the minor affairs of life; but the Lord shows in His dealings with Jacob that He will in no wise sanction or tolerate evil. All who endeavor to excuse or conceal their sins, and permit them to remain upon the books of heaven, unconfessed and unforgiven, will be overcome by Satan. The more exalted their profession and the more honorable the position which they hold, the more grievous is their course in the sight of God and the more sure the triumph of their great adversary. Those who delay a preparation for the day of God cannot obtain it in the time of trouble or at any subsequent time. The case of all such is hopeless. *The Great Controversy*, 620.

The Lord presented before Israel the results of holding communion with evil spirits, in the abominations of the Canaanites: they were without natural affection, idolaters, adulterers, murderers, and abominable by every corrupt thought and revolting practice. Men do not know their own hearts; for "the heart is deceitful above all things, and desperately wicked." Jeremiah 17:9. But God understands the tendencies of the depraved nature of man. Then, as now, Satan was watching to bring about conditions favorable to rebellion, that the people of Israel might make themselves as abhorrent to God as were the Canaanites. The adversary of souls is ever on the alert to open channels for the unrestrained flow of evil in us; for he desires that we may be ruined, and be condemned before God. *Patriarchs and Prophets*, 688.

Satan is ever ready to take advantage of the weaknesses and infirmities of men to suit his own purposes. He is a wily adversary, and has outgeneraled many whose purposes were good to benefit the cause of God with their means. Some have neglected the work that God has given them to do in appropriating their means. And while they are negligent in securing to the cause of God the means that He has lent them, Satan comes in and turns that means into his own ranks. *Testimonies for the Church*, Volume Two, 675.

In the wilderness of temptation, Satan, the adversary of souls, presented before Christ the glories of this world and said: "If Thou therefore wilt worship me, all shall be Thine." The Saviour repulsed Satan; but how easily is man seduced by the representations of the great enemy! Many are charmed with the attractions of the world; they serve mammon rather than God, and so lose their souls. *Testimonies for the Church, Volume Five*, 481.

Some who profess to love Christ, cherish cruel thoughts against others; and these thoughts, with their baleful influence, flow to the world in their words. All such are more closely allied to the great deceiver than to him who said, "Blessed are the peacemakers." Satan rules the tongues of all who give themselves into his keeping, filling the heart with envy and jealousy, and prompting the false whisper which so often causes untold misery. Those who lend themselves to his service do a work which makes him rejoice; but the angels of God weep as they see the evil that is wrought. Could those who thus give themselves up to mischief-making see how well pleasing their course of action is to the adversary of souls, they would say with the psalmist: "Deliver my soul, O Lord, from lying lips, and from a deceitful tongue. What shall be given unto thee? or what shall be done unto thee, thou false tongue? Sharp arrows of the mighty, with coals of juniper." *Advent Review and Sabbath Herald*, 2-16-97.

The adversary of souls is not permitted to read the thoughts of men; but he is a keen observer, and he marks the words; he takes account of actions, and skillfully adapts his temptations to meet the cases of those who place themselves in his power. If we would labor to repress sinful thoughts and feelings, giving them no expression in words or actions, Satan would be defeated; for he could not prepare his specious temptations to meet the case. But how often do professed Christians, by their lack of self-control, open the door to the adversary of souls! Divisions, and even bitter dissensions which would disgrace any worldly community, are common in the churches, because there is so little effort to control wrong feelings, and to repress every word that Satan can take advantage of. As soon as an alienation of feeling arises, the matter is spread before Satan for his inspection, and the opportunity given for him to use his serpent-like wisdom and skill in dividing and destroying the church. There is great loss in every dissension. Personal friends of both parties take sides with their respective favorites, and thus the breach is widened. A house divided against itself cannot stand. Criminations and recriminations are engendered and multiplied. Satan and his angels are actively at work to secure a harvest from seed thus sown. Worldlings look on, and jeeringly exclaim, "Behold how these Christians hate one another! If this is religion, we do not want it." And they look upon themselves and their irreligious characters with great satisfaction. Thus they are confirmed in their impenitence, and Satan exults at his success. *Advent Review and Sabbath Herald*, 3-22-87.

...Satan is preparing his deceptions, that in his last campaign against the people of God they may not understand that it is he. 2 Corinthians 11:14: "And no marvel; for Satan himself is transformed into an angel of light." While some deceived souls are advocating that he does not exist, he is taking them captive, and is working through them to a great extent. Satan knows better than God's people the power that they can have over him when their strength is in Christ. When they humbly entreat the mighty Conqueror for help, the weakest believer in the truth, relying firmly upon Christ, can successfully repulse Satan and all his host. He is too cunning to come openly, boldly, with his temptations; for then the drowsy energies of the Christian would arouse, and he would rely upon the strong and mighty Deliverer. But he comes in unperceived, and works in disguise through the children of disobedience who profess Godliness. *Testimonies for the Church*, Volume One, 341.

Chapter 10

OUR ADVERSARY THE DEVIL

A compassionate Creator, in yearning pity for Lucifer and his followers, was seeking to draw them back from the abyss of ruin into which they were about to plunge. But His mercy was misinterpreted. Lucifer pointed to the long-suffering of God as an evidence of his own superiority, an indication that the King of the universe would yet accede to his terms. If the angels would stand firmly with him, he declared, they could yet gain all that they desired. He persistently defended his own course, and fully committed himself to the great controversy against his Maker. Thus it was that Lucifer, "the light bearer," the sharer of God's glory, the attendant of His throne, by transgression became Satan, "the adversary" of God and holy beings and the destroyer of those whom Heaven had committed to his guidance and guardianship. *Patriarchs and Prophets*, 39, 40.

The ownership of the world belongs to Christ by creation and redemption. "God so loved the world, that he gave his only begotten Son, that whosoever believeth in him should not perish, but have everlasting life." In the work of redemption each one is called upon to be an agent for Christ. The apostle says, "Ye are laborers together with God." But Satan also employs men as his agents, and we are either workers together with God or with the enemy of our souls. The Devil is the adversary of God and man. Peter says, "Be sober, be vigilant; because your adversary the Devil, as a roaring lion, walketh about, seeking whom he may devour: whom resist steadfast in the faith, knowing that the same afflictions are accomplished in your brethren that are in the world." Satan is the tempter. He is the serpent that wounds and bruises the souls of men. He is a liar, an accuser of the brethren, He is a deceiver, and doeth great wonders, and appears in angel robes of light, that if possible he may deceive the very elect. Who will enlist in the warfare against the powerful foe that is seeking to insnare souls? Who will stand forth, and say intelligently, "We are laborers together with God?" Who will build upon the foundation that has been laid, which is Jesus Christ?... *Advent Review and Sabbath Herald*, 3-06-94

Christian friends, do not be deceived by the fast-spreading delusion that Satan has no existence. Just as surely as we have a personal Saviour, we have also a personal adversary, cruel and cunning, who ever watches our steps, and plots to lead us astray. Wherever the opinion is entertained that he does not exist, there he is most busy. When we least suspect his presence, he is gaining advantage over us. I feel alarmed as I see so many yielding to his power while they know it not. Did they but see their danger, they would flee to Christ, the sinner's refuge. They would resist the wiles of the adversary. They would pray much for wisdom, grace, and strength, and would seek most earnestly to overcome every evil trait of character. They would walk in the path that Jesus trod, and shun that which Satan urges them to choose. *The Signs of the Times*, 8-19-86.

In the world there are false theories which deny the existence of Satan, or make him to hideous as to encourage doubt of his existence. The world has no just conception of Satan. He is not thought of as the prince of the world, the general of a vast rebellion, a being logical and philosophical, possessing a powerful intellect. But thus it is. The adversary of God and leader in the great controversy waged against the world's Redeemer, his deceptive powers have been sharpened by constant practice; and in the final crisis he will deceive to their own ruin those who do not now seek to understand his methods of working. *Advent Review and Sabbath Herald*, 7-16-01.

The sinner is exposed to eternal death, until he finds a hiding place in Christ; and as loitering and carelessness might rob the fugitive of his only chance for life, so delays and indifference may prove the ruin of the soul. Satan, the great adversary, is on the track of every transgressor of God's holy law, and he who is not sensible of his danger, and does not earnestly seek shelter in the eternal refuge, will fall a prey to the destroyer. *Patriarchs and Prophets*, 517.

It is not enough to merely profess to believe the truth. All the soldiers of the cross of Christ virtually obligate themselves to enter the crusade against the adversary of souls, to condemn wrong and sustain righteousness. But the message of the True Witness reveals the fact that a terrible deception is upon our people, which makes it necessary to come to them with warnings, to break their spiritual slumber, and arouse them to decided action. *Testimonies for the Church*, Volume Three, 254.

There are Christians who think and speak altogether too much about the power of Satan. They think of their adversary, they pray about him, they talk about him, and he looms up greater and greater in their imagination. It is true that Satan is a powerful being; but, thank God, we have a mighty Saviour, who cast out the evil one from heaven. Satan is pleased when we magnify his power. Why not talk of Jesus? Why not magnify His power and His love? *The Desire of Ages*, 493.

Yet we have a work to do to resist temptation. Those who would not fall a prey to Satan's devices must guard well the avenues of the soul; they must avoid reading, seeing, or hearing that which will suggest impure thoughts. The mind should not be left to wander at random upon every subject that the adversary of souls may suggest. "Girding up the loins of your mind," says the apostle Peter, "Be sober, . . . not fashioning yourselves according to your former lusts in . . . your ignorance: but like as He which called you is holy, be ye yourselves also holy in all manner of living." 1 Peter 1:13–15, R.V. Says Paul, "Whatsoever things are true, whatsoever things are honest, whatsoever things are just, whatsoever things are pure, whatsoever things are lovely, whatsoever things are of good report; if there be any virtue, and if there be any praise, think on these things."

Philippians 4:8. This will require earnest prayer and unceasing watchfulness. We must be aided by the abiding influence of the Holy Spirit, which will attract the mind upward, and habituate it to dwell on pure and holy things. And we must give diligent study to the word of God. "Wherewithal shall a young man cleanse his way? by taking heed thereto according to Thy word." "Thy word," says the psalmist, "have I hid in mine heart, that I might not sin against Thee." Psalm 119:9, 11. *Patriarchs and Prophets*, 460.

Shall we look at our sins, and begin to mourn, and say, I have done wrong, and I cannot come to God with any degree of confidence? Does not the Bible say, "If we confess our sins, he is faithful and just to forgive us our sins, and to cleanse us from all unrighteousness"? It is a proper thing for us to have a realization of the terrible character of sin. It was sin that caused Christ to suffer an ignominious death on Calvary. But while we should understand that sin is a terrible thing, we should not listen to the voice of our adversary, who says, "You have sinned, and you have no right to claim the promises of God." You should say to the adversary, It is written, "If any man sin, we have an advocate with the Father, Jesus Christ the righteous." I am so glad that God has made a provision whereby we may know that he does pardon our transgressions! We do not believe in God as we should, and I have thought that this unbelief is our greatest sin. The psalmist says, "I acknowledged my sin unto thee, and mine iniquity have I not hid. I said, I will confess my transgressions unto the Lord; and thou forgavest the iniquity of my sin." "Come, ye children, hearken unto me: I will teach you the fear of the Lord. What man is he that desireth life, and loveth many days, that he may see good? Keep thy tongue from evil, and thy lips from speaking guile. Depart from evil, and do good; seek peace, and pursue it. The eyes of the Lord are upon the righteous, and his ears are open unto their cry. . . . The Lord is nigh unto them that are of a broken heart; and saveth such as be of a contrite spirit." This is the kind of experience that we should have. *Advent Review and Sabbath Herald*, 5-19-96.

My brother, my sister, open the door of the heart to receive Jesus. Invite him into the soul-temple. Help each other to overcome the obstacles which enter the married life of all. You will have a fierce conflict to overcome your adversary the devil, and if you expect God to help you in this battle, you must both unite in deciding to overcome, to seal your lips against speaking any words of wrong, even if you have to fall upon your knees and cry aloud, "Lord, rebuke the adversary of my soul." *The Adventist Home*, 119, 120.

My brethren and sisters, old and young, when you have an hour of leisure open the Bible and store the mind with its precious truths. When engaged in labor, guard the mind, keep it stayed upon God, talk less and meditate more. Remember, "Every idle word that men shallspeak, they shall give account thereof in the day of judgment." Matthew 12:36. Let your words be select; this will close a door against the adversary of souls. Let your day be entered upon with prayer; work as in God's sight. His angels are ever by your side, making a record of your words, your deportment, and the manner in which your work is done. *Counsels on Health*, 415, 416.

The widow's prayer, "Avenge me"—"do me justice" (R.V.)—"of mine adversary," represents the prayer of God's children. Satan is their great adversary. He is the "accuser of our brethren," who accuses them before God day and night. (Rev. 12:10.) He is continually working to misrepresent and accuse, to deceive and destroy the people of God. And it is for deliverance from the power of Satan and his agents that in this parable Christ teaches His disciples to pray. *Christ's Object Lessons*, 166.

The prayer, "Do me justice of mine adversary," applies not only to Satan, but to the agencies whom he instigates to misrepresent, to tempt, and to destroy the people of God. Those who have decided to obey the commandments of God will understand by experience that they have adversaries who are controlled by a power from beneath. Such adversaries beset Christ at every step, how constantly and determinedly no human being can ever know. Christ's disciples, like their Master, are followed by continual temptation. *Christ's Object Lessons*, 170.

I saw that the cause of God was not progressing as it might and as it should. Ministers fail to take hold of the work with that energy, devotion, and decided perseverance which the importance of the work demands. They have a vigilant adversary to contend with whose diligence and perseverance are untiring. The feeble effort of ministers and people can bear no comparison with those of their adversary, the devil. On one side are the ministers who battle for the right and have the help of God and holy angels. They should be strong and valiant, and wholly devoted to the cause in which they are engaged, having no separate interest. They should not be entangled with the things of this life, that they may please Him who hath chosen them to be soldiers. *Testimonies for the Church*, Volume One, 467.

"Be sober, be vigilant; because your adversary the devil, as a roaring lion, walketh about, seeking whom he may devour." Verse 8. He is on the playground, watching your amusements, and catching every soul whom he finds off guard, sowing his seeds in human hearts, and gaining control of human minds. He is present in every exercise in the schoolroom. Those students who allow their minds to be deeply excited over games are not in the best condition to receive the instruction, the counsel, the reproof, most essential for them. *Counsels to Parents, Teachers, and Students*, 283.

Our great adversary has agents that are constantly hunting for an opportunity to destroy souls, as a lion hunts his prey. Shun them, young man; for, while they appear to be your friends, they will slyly introduce evil ways and practices. They flatter you with their lips, and offer to help and guide you; but their steps take hold on hell. If you listen to their counsel, it may be the turning point in your life. One safeguard removed from conscience, the indulgence of one evil habit, a single neglect of the high claims of duty, may be the beginning of a course of deception that will pass you into the ranks of those who are serving Satan, while you are all the time professing to love God and His cause. A moment of thoughtlessness, a single misstep, may turn the whole current of your lives in the wrong direction. And you may never know what caused your ruin until the sentence is pronounced: "Depart from Me, ye that work iniquity." *Colporteur Ministry*, 52.

The course of Christ in dealing even with the adversary of souls, should be an example to us in all our intercourse with others, never to bring a railing accusation against any; much less should we employ harshness or severity toward those who may be as anxious to know the right way as we are ourselves. *Counsels to Writers and Editors*, 59.

The apostle gives us his experience and the experience of his fellow laborers in their work. "We are troubled on every side," he says; "yet not distressed; we are perplexed, but not in despair; persecuted, but not forsaken; cast down, but not destroyed; always bearing about in the body the dying of the Lord Jesus, that the life also of Jesus might be made manifest in our body." If we work the works of Christ, the mind will gather strength and firmness to resist the adversary of souls. The apostle says, "Think it not strange concerning the fiery trial which is to try you, as though some strange, thing happened unto you." "Ye are in heaviness through manifold temptations: that the trial of your faith, being much more precious than of gold that perisheth, though it be tried with fire, might be found unto praise and honor and glory at the appearing of Jesus Christ." "Wherefore let them that suffer according to the will of God commit the keeping of their souls to him in well-doing, as unto a faithful Creator." "Humble yourselves therefore under the mighty hand of God, that he may exalt you in due time: casting all your care upon him; for he careth for you. Be sober, be vigilant; because your adversary the devil, as a roaring lion, walketh about, seeking whom he may devour: whom resist steadfast in the faith, knowing that the same afflictions are accomplished in your brethren that are in the world." *The Youth's Instructor,* 11-09-99

Higher education is an experimental knowledge of the plan of salvation, and this knowledge is secured by earnest and diligent study of the Scriptures. Such an education will renew the mind and transform the character, restoring the image of God in the soul. It will fortify the mind against the deceptive whisperings of the adversary, and enable us to understand the voice of God. It will teach the learner to become a co-worker with Jesus Christ, to dispel the moral darkness about him, and bring light and knowledge to men. It is the simplicity of true godliness—our passport from the preparatory school of earth to the higher school above. *Counsels to Parents, Teachers, and Students,* 11.

The student who yields to temptation weakens his influence for good, and he who by a wrong course of action becomes the agent of the adversary of souls must render to God an account for the part he has acted in laying stumbling blocks in the way of others. Why should students link themselves with the great apostate? Why should they become his agents to tempt others? Rather, why should they not study to help and encourage their fellow students and their teachers? It is their privilege to help their teachers bear the burdens and meet the perplexities that Satan would make discouragingly heavy and trying. They may create an atmosphere that will be helpful, exhilarating. Every student may enjoy the consciousness that he has stood on Christ's side, showing respect for order, diligence, and obedience, and refusing to lend one jot of his ability or influence to the great enemy of all that is good and uplifting. *Counsels to Parents, Teachers, and Students,* 224, 225.

Thus the question, "Who is my neighbor?" is forever answered. Christ has shown that our neighbor does not mean merely one of the church or faith to which we belong. It has no reference to race, color, or class distinction. Our neighbor is every person who needs our help. Our neighbor is every soul who is wounded and bruised by the adversary. Our neighbor is everyone who is the property of God. *The Desire of Ages*, 503.

Our work is to toil in the vineyard of the Lord, not merely for ourselves, but for the good of others. Our influence is a blessing or a curse to others. We are here to form perfect characters for heaven. We have something to do besides repining and murmuring at God's providences, and writing bitter things against ourselves. Our adversary will not allow us to rest. It we are indeed God's children we shall be harassed and sorely beset, and we need not expect that Satan or those under his influence will treat us well. But there are angels who excel in strength who will be with us in all our conflicts if we will only be faithful. Christ conquered Satan in our behalf in the wilderness of temptation. He is mightier than Satan, and He will shortly bruise him under our feet. *Testimonies for the Church*, Volume Three, 526.

The Lord declares, "The message is to go forth in words of solemn warning. Nothing that will hinder the clear presentation of the message is to be introduced into your plans. Repeat the message. The wickedness in the cities is increasing; the adversary has great influence over men, because My people did not open their hearts to realize their responsibility. Tell My people to take up their work and proclaim the message. They are to speak and work in the simplicity of true godliness, and My Spirit will make the impression on hearts. Let the true note of warning be sounded. My angel shall go before you if you will be sanctified through the truth." *Letter 88*, 1910; *Counsels to Writers and Editors*, 23.

...Often He [Jesus] met those who had drifted under Satan's control, and who had no power to break from his snare. To such a one, discouraged, sick, tempted, and fallen, Jesus would speak words of tenderest pity, words that were needed and could be understood. Others He met who were fighting a hand-to-hand battle with the adversary of souls. These He encouraged to persevere, assuring them that they would win;

for angels of God were on their side, and would give them the victory. Those whom He thus helped were convinced that here was One in whom they could trust with perfect confidence. He would not betray the secrets they poured into His sympathizing ear. *Desire of Ages*, 91, 92.

God's healing power runs all through nature. If a tree is cut, if a human being is wounded or breaks a bone, nature begins at once to repair the injury. Even before the need exists, the healing agencies are in readiness; and as soon as a part is wounded, every energy is bent to the work of restoration. So it is in the spiritual realm. Before sin created the need, God had provided the remedy. Every soul that yields to temptation is wounded, bruised, by the adversary; but whenever there is sin, there is the Saviour. It is Christ's work "to heal the brokenhearted, to preach deliverance to the captives,...to set at liberty them that are bruised." Luke 4:18. *Education*, 113.

My sister, Christ has committed to you the sacred work of teaching His commandments to your children. In order to be fitted for this work, you must yourself live in obedience to all His precepts. Cultivate a watchful observance of every word and action. Guard most diligently your words. Overcome all hastiness of temper; for impatience, if manifested, will help the adversary to make the home life disagreeable and unpleasant for your children. *Child Guidance*, 68.

Fallen man is Satan's lawful captive. The mission of Christ was to rescue him from the power of his great adversary. Man is naturally inclined to follow Satan's suggestions, and he cannot successfully resist so terrible a foe unless Christ, the mighty Conqueror, dwells in him, guiding his desires, and giving him strength. God alone can limit the power of Satan. He is going to and fro in the earth, and walking up and down in it. He is not off his watch for a single moment, through fear of losing an opportunity to destroy souls. It is important that God's people understand this, that they may escape his snares... *Testimonies for the Church*, Volume One, 341.

The example of Christ shows us that our only hope of victory is in continual resistance of Satan's attacks. He who triumphed over the adversary of souls in the conflict of temptation understands Satan's power over the race and has conquered him in our behalf. As an overcomer He has given us the advantage of His victory, that in our efforts to resist the temptations of Satan we may unite our weakness to His strength, our worthlessness to His merits. And, sustained by His enduring might under strong temptation, we may resist in His all-powerful name and overcome as He overcame. *Testimonies for the Church*, Volume Three, 480.

The church of Christ may be fitly compared to an army. The life of every soldier is one of toil, hardship, and danger. On every hand are vigilant foes, led on by the prince of the powers of darkness, who never slumbers and never deserts his post. Whenever a Christian is off his guard, this powerful adversary makes a sudden and violent attack. Unless the members of the church are active and vigilant, they will be overcome by his devices. *Testimonies for the Church*, Volume Five, 394.

At this time of general intemperance and worldliness, every true Christian will have a battle to fight to practice the principles of truth as well as to assent to them. It is genuine, personal experience in the Christian life, the Christian warfare, that ministers of the gospel need. The Captain of our salvation calls for witnesses fresh from the field of action. Those who have been fiercely assaulted by the enemies of truth and the adversary of souls, and who have conducted themselves as did Jesus in his hour of trial, will have a testimony to bear which will thrill the hearts of the hearers. They will indeed be witnesses for Jesus. *Second Advent Review and Sabbath Herald*, 12-20-81.

Jesus does not present to his followers the hope of attaining earthly glory and riches, and of having a life free from trial; but he presents to them the privilege of walking with their Master in the path of suffering, self-denial, and reproach because the world knoweth them not. He does not hold out to them any false hopes of living at ease. He takes them to an eminence and shows them the confederacy of evil arrayed against them under the leadership of Satan, the great adversary. But while showing to them the foes with which they will have to contend, he also assures them that they will not have to fight alone. They will have the fellowship of heavenly intelligences, and though the world lieth in darkness, they are to catch the radiance from the throne of God, and diffuse the light of heaven amid the moral darkness of the world. *Advent Review and Sabbath Herald*, 11-06-94.

Christ will be constantly laboring for your salvation. Angels will be commissioned to guard you from the devices of the adversary, and to minister to all your needs. And the object of all this abundant solicitude must, on his part, depart from all iniquity, and perfect holiness in the fear of God. He must watch and pray. He must fight the good fight of faith, resist the devil that he may flee from him, and endure hardness as a good soldier of the cross of Christ. He has to wage a constant conflict with unseen foes, and only through Christ can he come off victorious. He must cultivate courage to surmount the difficulties obstructing his pathway, and build up a character of integrity and virtue, representing to the world the character of his Redeemer. *The Signs of the Times*, 3-23-88.

Chapter 11

LUCIFER'S LESSON

Satan's rebellion was to be a lesson to the universe through all coming ages, a perpetual testimony to the nature and terrible results of sin. The working out of Satan's rule, its effects upon both men and angels, would show what must be the fruit of setting aside the divine authority. It would testify that with the existence of God's government and His law is bound up the well-being of all the creatures He has made. Thus the history of this terrible experiment of rebellion was to be perpetual safeguard to all holy intelligences, to prevent them from being deceived as to the nature of transgression, to save them from committing sin and suffering its punishments. *The Great Controversy*, 499.

There are those who say, "Give me Christ, but I want nothing of the law." They talk of the grace of Christ, but they know not the meaning of grace; for God does not use His grace to make void the law. Satan has confused their minds, leading them to look upon the law as a yoke of bondage, a hindrance to spirituality. They talk of faith, but they know not the meaning of the word; for faith is never found apart from truth. The peace which they boast their faith gives them is but self-righteous confidence. Let no one claim that he has been accepted by Christ, and is living without sin, while at the same time he is, like Lucifer, waging war against God's law, aiding the enemy in the very work which he commenced in heaven and is carrying forward on this earth. *The Signs of the Times*, 7-31-01.

We shall have false sentiments to meet. Never, never can we afford to place confidence in human greatness as some have done, looking to man as the angels in heaven looked to the rebellious Lucifer, and losing the sense of the presence of Christ and God. *Manuscript Releases*, Volume Twenty-one, 419.

While Lucifer counted it a thing to be grasped to be equal with God, Christ, the Exalted One, "made Himself of no reputation, and took upon Him the form of a servant, and was made in the likeness of men: and being found in fashion as a man, He humbled Himself, and became obedient unto death, even the death of the cross." Phil. 2:7, 8. Now the cross was just before Him; and His own disciples were so filled with self-seeking—the very principle of Satan's kingdom—that they could not enter into sympathy with their Lord, or even understand Him as He spoke of His humiliation for them. *The Desire of Ages*, 436.

I ask our people to study the twenty-eighth chapter of Ezekiel. The representation here made, while it refers primarily to Lucifer, the fallen angel, has yet a broader significance. Not one being, but a general movement, is described, and one that we shall witness. A faithful study of this chapter should lead those who are seeking for truth to walk in all the light that God has given to His people, lest they be deceived by the deceptions of these last days. (*Special Testimonies*, Series B, No. 17, p. 30); *S.D.A. Bible Commentary*, Vol. 4, 1162.

"None are too high to fall. Sin originated with Satan, who was next to Christ. Lucifer became the destroyer of those whom heaven had committed to his guardianship. Satan has a church in our world to-day. In his church are all the disaffected ones and the disloyal. All who harbor pride, ambition, vain-glory, or selfishness, will be found wanting when weighed in the balance of the Lord. We cannot of ourselves perfect a true moral character, but we can accept the righteousness of Christ. 'He that saith he abideth in Him ought himself also so to walk, even as He walked.'" (Australasian) *Union Conference Record*, 10-01-06.

Parents, will you awake to the God-given responsibility resting upon you? Never speak harshly or angrily to your children or to each other. God expects you, in spirit and word and act, to be representatives of him. He expects you to do what Christ would do were he in your place. Your words are to be well chosen, never showing impatience. You are to keep the tongue under restraint. Your lives are to reveal the sanctification of true godliness. Do not let Satan control your tongue. Be true missionaries in the home. Remember that the training you are giving your children is making them either Christlike in word and deed, or like the fallen angel, Lucifer, who, because he was determined to have his own way and be above Christ, was cast out of heaven. *Advent Review and Sabbath Herald*, 12-22-10.

The fallen angel whom God had made covering cherub, was ruined by his selfish, independent will. God had made him noble, had given him rich endowments. He gave him a high, responsible position. He asked of him nothing that was unreasonable. He was to administer the trust given him of God in a spirit of meekness and devotion, seeking to promote the glory of God, who had given him glory and beauty and loveliness. But Lucifer abode not in the truth. He fell from his integrity. Let everyone learn the lesson which he should learn from this wonderful history. *Sabbath-School Worker*, 03-01-93.

Munzer taught that all who would receive the Spirit must mortify the flesh, wear tattered clothing, neglect the body, be of a sad countenance, and, forsaking all their former associates, retire to desert places, and there entreat the favor of God. "Then, said he, "God will come and speak with us as formerly he spoke with Abraham, Isaac, and Jacob. If he were not to do so, he would not deserve our attention." Thus was this deluded man, like Lucifer himself, making terms for God, and refusing to acknowledge his authority unless he should comply with these terms. *The Signs of the Times*, 10-25-83.

To the Romanist the Bible is a forbidden book, because it plainly reveals the errors of the Roman system; and whoever searches the Bible with an enlightened understanding, cannot long be in harmony with Romanism. He who searches the Bible to understand the truth, will find no authority in the word of God for the assumption of power on the part of popes and cardinals. There is no word of God that sanctions their assumed superiority or supremacy over their people, as there is no word to sanction the claim that Lucifer made in heaven of superiority over Christ. The claim of the Papacy to superiority is made under the influence of the first great usurper, who so persistently urged his right to supremacy over the host of God. Through the Dark Ages,—that long night of ignorance and superstition,—the claim of the Papacy to superiority and supremacy was conceded by emperors and kings, although God had sanctioned no such concession, and raised up men to dispute the claim, and to break the Romish yoke from the church of God. Through his appointed agencies God summoned the church to reassert her independence, and in the strength of God she stood forth in the liberty wherewith Christ had made her free. She broke away from the papal yoke, and with the word of God in her hand, met the giant evil of Romanism, even as David met Goliath in the name of heaven, using his sling and a few pebblestones. The defier of Israel was slain before the man of faith; and while men cling to the word of the Lord, they cannot affiliate with the great system of error. *The Signs of the Times*, 2-19-94.

And I was shown from the first that the Lord had given neither Elders Daniells nor Prescott the burden of this work. Should Satan's wiles be brought in, should this "Daily" be such a great matter as to be brought in to confuse minds and hinder the advancement of the work at this important period of time? It should not, whatever may be. This subject should not be introduced, for the spirit that would be brought in would be forbidding, and Lucifer is watching every movement. Satanic agencies would commence his work and there would be confusion brought into our ranks. You have no call to hunt up the difference of opinion that is not a testing question; but your silence is eloquence. I have the matter all plainly before me. If the devil could involve any one of our own people on these subjects, as he has proposed to do, Satan's cause would triumph. Now the work without delay is to be taken up and not a [difference] of opinion expressed. *Manuscript Releases*, Volume Twenty, 18.

When a man takes the position that when he has once made a decision he must stand by it, and never to alter his decision, he is on the same ground as was Lucifer when he rebelled against God. He held his plans regarding the government of heaven as an exalted, unchangeable theory. *S.D.A. Bible Commentary*, Vol. Three, 1161.

Now I have not been able to sleep after twelve o'clock for two nights because the case of Elder Cottrell has been presented to me. The Lord will use Elder Cottrell if he will give up the idea that plans he may suggest are infallible, never to be revoked. This understanding is an erroneous idea. God does not endorse it. This is the position that Lucifer took. He was next to Christ in the heavenly courts, but decided that he was entitled to a higher position. Read and understand Ezekiel 28:11–18. This matter has been opened to me. When the Lord sought to correct him, he would not be corrected; and when any man in all our ranks shall not be willing to yield up his own way, but will persistently choose to follow his own judgment, carrying the idea that his judgment is unchangeable, he claims infallibility. The Lord has no more any use for him unless he changes his ideas. *Manuscript Releases*, Volume Twenty, 226.

Wisdom, intellect, power—these are not God. But God is the Author of all wisdom, all grace, all power. God gave Lucifer his power and wisdom, yet this intelligence was not God Himself. We are to know God as He is revealed in His marvelous works. Who by searching can find out God? This is not part of our work....God's character is expressed in the Ten Commandments. To know God as He is—this is the science of all goodness and truth and righteousness. We must obey every expression of His character as revealed in His law. *The Upward Look*, 347.

Jesus marked out in a plain way the line of conduct that we all should pursue. We are to love God supremely, and our neighbors as ourselves. The question asked by the lawyer is of importance to each one of us, and the answer is plain and decided, so that no man need walk in darkness, because he has the light. The whole duty of man is comprised in keeping the first four and the last six commandments. The Spirit that prompts men to reveal in life the love of God will also make a man an obedient member of the heavenly family. If men love worldly things, name, position, wealth, or any object that leads them to forget God, they love that which makes them idolaters. Nothing should be permitted to so hold the affections that God is thrust out of the mind. The second commandment will be easily disobeyed if the first is not kept. Supreme love of God will sanctify the affections, and the fruit of love to God will be love to mankind. Those who have been tested and proved on this matter of loving others as themselves, will be pronounced meet for an inheritance with the saints in light. They will not become exalted, as did Lucifer in the courts of light. They will not create rebellion in heaven, because another has a brighter crown than they have. Heaven will be the home of the pure and undefiled, and those who reach that home of joy will feel rich, receiving a reward that they do not in the least feel that they deserve. *The Signs of the Times*, 7-02-94.

In His Word the Lord declared what He would do for Israel if they would obey His voice. But the leaders of the people yielded to the temptations of Satan, and God could not give them the blessings He designed them to have, because they did not obey His voice but listened to the voice and policy of Lucifer. This experience will be repeated in the last years of the history of the people of God, who have been established by His grace and power. Men whom He has greatly honored will in the closing scenes of this earth's history pattern after ancient Israel. *Manuscript Releases*, Volume Thirteen, 379.

Let the followers of Christ do all that is possible to teach repentance toward God and faith toward our Lord Jesus

Christ. One soul gained brings joy to the Father and to the Son, and there is rejoicing in the presence of the angels of heaven, and an anthem of praise goes up from countless harps and voices through the heavenly courts. Those who break the law of God, and teach others to break God's commandments, are not following Jesus, who says, "I have kept my Father's commandments;" they are following another leader. It was Christ's own voice that proclaimed on Mount Sinai the Ten Commandments, and he will not countermand his statutes. Satan in his rebellion in heaven sought to find some flaw in the law of God, in order to support his argument that the law of God must be changed; but his efforts were in vain. He did not succeed, and after he had deceived thousands of angels, and had drawn them to his side, he was cast out of heaven. But the law of God was not changed in one jot or tittle. God is wise and unchangeable, and those who flatter themselves that they can find a safer rule of life than that which God has given, are deceived by the same delusions that led the angels of heaven to join the ranks of Lucifer in questioning the authority of God's law and the justice of his government. *The Signs of the Times*, 11-14-95.

Shall Christ be compelled to bear continually the shameful infirmities of His people because they accept the false sentiments proceeding from the first traitor in the heavenly courts? If the angels were deceived by Lucifer's ingenious methods of misrepresenting God, if Adam and Eve were deceived by his declaration that God was withholding from them the higher education that would make them as gods, is there not danger that men today will be deceived? Please read the first chapter of Patriarchs and Prophets and see if the precious truths contained in this book are not given by the Lord to protect His people from deceptions that are urged upon them just now. *Manuscript Releases*, Volume Ten, 162, 163.

Pantheistic ideas regarding God in nature are framed by Lucifer, the fallen angel. The strange part of the matter is that these ideas have been accepted by so many as beautiful truth. But that which they think is light will lead them into dense darkness. It is a distinguishing feature of the experience of Seventh-day Adventists to give glory to God. When we give glory to human agencies, when we have unlimited confidence in man, speaking of the excellence that we suppose him to possess, we worship we know not what. Let God be exalted. Let frail, erring human beings humble themselves before Him.... *The Upward Look*, 336.

The Gospel is the voice of duty and the voice of God. What is meant by a failure to obey its principles is shown in the history of Satan, who for his disobedience was cast out of heaven. The highest gifts that could be bestowed in a created being were given to Lucifer, the covering cherub. Before his fall he was a glorious being, occupying a position next to Christ in the heavenly courts. But in seeking to be equal with God he brought upon himself irretrievable ruin. *The Signs of the Times*, 7-10-01.

Christians are engaged in a warfare. The church militant is not the church triumphant. The followers of Christ, marching toward Zion, must fight at every step. His adversary is the one who once stood in the heavenly courts as the first of the covering cherubs. The beams of glory enshrouding the eternal God, once rested constantly upon him. But, not content with his position, tho honored above the heavenly host, he began to covet the glory with which the Father had invested the Son. Lucifer desired to be first in heaven. Thus he introduced sin into the universe. Entering the Garden of Eden after his expulsion from heaven, he succeeded in deceiving our first parents. Ever since he has claimed this world. Declaring that no human-being can keep the law of God's kingdom, he claims all men as his subjects. *The Signs of the Times*, 6-10-03

We are living in the time of the end, when the judgments of God are in the land. Signs on every hand show that the agencies of evil are strengthening. Lucifer and his servants are working with unceasing activity. In this time of peril the people who keep the Sabbath of the fourth commandment are to be awake to the situation, prepared to resist the attacks of the enemy. While wickedness abounds on every hand, God's people are to be fully controlled by the Holy Spirit. Greater solemnity and earnestness should be brought into the work. All light and trifling words should be left unspoken. Believers should speak and act as a people who realize the solemn meaning of the events taking place. *Australasian Record,* 4-15-12.

Chapter 12

SATAN'S FINAL MOVES

The great controversy between good and evil will increase in intensity to the very close of time. In all ages the wrath of Satan has been manifested against the church of Christ; and God has bestowed His grace and Spirit upon His people to strengthen them to stand against the power of the evil one. When the apostles of Christ were to bear His gospel to the world and to record it for all future ages, they were especially endowed with the enlightenment of the Spirit. But as the church approaches her final deliverance, Satan is to work with greater power. He comes down "having great wrath, because he knoweth that he hath but a short time." Revelation 12:12. He will work "with all power and signs and lying wonders." 2 Thessalonians 2:9. For six thousand years that mastermind that once was highest among the angels of God has been wholly bent to the work of deception and ruin. And all the depths of satanic skill and subtlety acquired, all the cruelty developed, during these struggles of the ages, will be brought to bear against God's people in the final conflict. And in this time of peril the followers of Christ are to bear to the world the warning of the Lord's second advent; and a people are to be prepared to stand before Him at His coming, "without spot, and blameless." 2 Peter 3:14. At this time the special endowment of divine grace and power is not less needful to the church than in apostolic days. *The Great Controversy*, ix, x.

The agencies of evil are combining their forces and consolidating. They are strengthening for the last great crisis. Great changes are soon to take place in our world, and the final movements will be rapid ones. *Testimonies for the Church*, Volume Nine, 11.

That the law which was spoken by God's own voice is faulty, that some specification has been set aside, is the claim which Satan now puts forward. It is the last great deception that he will bring upon the world. He needs not to assail the whole law; if he can lead men to disregard one precept, his purpose is gained. For "whosoever shall keep the whole law, and yet offend in one point, he is guilty of all." James 2:10. By consenting to break one precept, men are brought under Satan's power. By substituting human law for God's law, Satan will seek to control the world. This work is foretold in prophecy. Of the great apostate power which is the representative of Satan, it is declared, "He shall speak great words against the Most High, and shall wear out the saints of the Most High, and think to change times and laws: and they shall be given into his hand." Dan. 7:25. *The Desire of Ages*, 763.

Satan has long been preparing for his final effort to deceive the world. The foundation of his work was laid by the assurance given to Eve in Eden: "Ye shall not surely die." "In the day ye eat thereof, then your eyes shall be opened, and ye shall be as gods, knowing good and evil." Genesis 3:4, 5. Little by little he has prepared the way for his masterpiece of deception in the development of spiritualism. He has not yet reached the full accomplishment of his designs; but it will be reached in the last remnant of time. Says the prophet: "I saw three unclean spirits like frogs; . . . they are the spirits of devils, working miracles, which go forth unto the kings of the earth and of the whole world, to gather them to the battle of that great day of God Almighty." Revelation 16:13, 14. Except those who are kept by the power of God, through faith in His word, the whole world will be swept into the ranks of this delusion. The people are fast being lulled to a fatal security, to be awakened only by the outpouring of the wrath of God. *The Great Controversy*, 561, 562.

Before the final visitation of God's judgments upon the earth there will be among the people of the Lord such a revival of primitive godliness as has not been witnessed since apostolic times. The Spirit and power of God will be poured out upon His children. At that time many will separate themselves from those churches in which the love of this world has supplanted love for God and His word. Many, both of ministers and people, will gladly accept those great truths which God has caused to be proclaimed at this time to prepare a people for the Lord's second coming. The enemy of souls desires to hinder this work; and before the time for such a movement shall come, he will endeavor to prevent it by introducing a counterfeit. In those churches which he can bring under his deceptive power he will make it appear that God's special blessing is poured out; there will be manifest what is thought to be great religious interest. Multitudes will exult that God is working marvelously for them, when the work is that of another spirit. Under a religious guise, Satan will seek to extend his influence over the Christian world. *The Great Controversy*, 464.

It is impossible to estimate too largely the work that the Lord will accomplish through His proposed vessels in carrying out His mind and purpose. The things you have described as taking place in Indiana, the Lord has shown me would take place just before the close of probation. Every uncouth thing will be demonstrated. There will be shouting, with drums, music, and dancing. The senses of rational beings will become so confused that they cannot be trusted to make right decisions. And this is called the moving of the Holy Spirit.

The Holy Spirit never reveals itself in such methods, in such a bedlam of noise. This is an invention of Satan to cover up his ingenious methods for making of none effect the pure, sincere, elevating, ennobling, sanctifying truth for this time. Better never have the worship of God blended with music than to use musical instruments to do the work which last January was represented to me would be brought into our camp meetings. The truth for this time needs nothing of this kind in its work of converting souls. A bedlam of noise shocks the senses and perverts that which if conducted aright might be a blessing. The powers of satanic agencies blend with the din and noise, to have a carnival, and this is termed the Holy Spirit's working. *Selected Messages*, Book Two, 36.

The enemy of souls has sought to bring in the supposition that a great reformation was to take place among Seventh-day Adventists, and that this reformation would consist in giving up the doctrines which stand as the pillars of our faith, and engaging in a process of reorganization. Were this reformation to take place, what would result? The principles of truth that God in His wisdom has given to the remnant church, would be discarded. Our religion would be changed. The fundamental principles that have sustained the work for the last fifty years would be accounted as error. A new organization would be established. Books of a new order would be written. A system of intellectual philosophy would be introduced. The founders of this system would go into the cities, and do a wonderful work. The Sabbath of course, would be lightly regarded, as also the God who created it. Nothing would be allowed to stand in the way of the new movement. The leaders would teach that virtue is better than vice, but God being removed, they would place their dependence on human power, which, without God, is worthless. Their foundation would be built on the sand, and storm and tempest would sweep away the structure. *Selected Messages*, Book One, 204, 205.

As the crowning act in the great drama of deception, Satan himself will personate Christ. The church has long professed to look to the Saviour's advent as the consummation of her hopes. Now the great deceiver will make it appear that Christ has come. In different parts of the earth, Satan will manifest himself among men as a majestic being of dazzling brightness, resembling the description of the Son of God given by John in the Revelation. Revelation 1:13–15. The glory that surrounds him is unsurpassed by anything that mortal eyes have yet beheld. The shout of triumph rings out upon the air: "Christ has come! Christ has come!" The people prostrate themselves in adoration before him, while he lifts up his hands and pronounces a blessing upon them, as Christ blessed His disciples when He was upon the earth. His voice is soft and subdued, yet full of melody. In gentle, compassionate tones he presents some of the same gracious, heavenly truths which the Saviour uttered; he heals the diseases of the people, and then, in his assumed character of Christ, he claims to have changed the Sabbath to Sunday, and commands all to hallow the day which he has blessed. He declares that those who persist in keeping holy the seventh day are blaspheming his name by refusing to listen to his angels sent to them with light and truth. This is the strong, almost overmastering delusion. Like the Samaritans who were deceived by Simon Magus, the multitudes, from the least to the greatest, give heed to these sorceries, saying: This is "the great power of God." Acts 8:10. *The Great Controversy*, 624.

The very last deception of Satan will be to make of none effect the testimony of the Spirit of God. "Where there is no vision, the people perish" (Proverbs 29:18). Satan will work ingeniously, in different ways and through different agencies, to unsettle the confidence of God's remnant people in the true testimony. He will bring in spurious visions to mislead, and will mingle the false with the true, and so disgust people that they will regard everything that bears the name of visions as a species of fanaticism; but honest souls, by contrasting false and true, will be enabled to distinguish between them. *Manuscript Releases*, Volume Ten, 311.

Chapter 13

SATAN'S DEFEAT

Jesus began His work by breaking Satan's power over the suffering. He restored the sick to health, gave sight to the blind, and healed the lame, causing them to leap for joy and to glorify God. He restored to health those who had been infirm and bound by Satan's cruel power many years. With gracious words He comforted the weak, the trembling, and the desponding. The feeble, suffering ones whom Satan held in triumph, Jesus wrenched from his grasp, bringing to them soundness of body and great joy and happiness. He raised the dead to life, and they glorified God for the mighty display of His power. He wrought mightily for all who believed on Him. *Early Writings*, 159, 160.

Jesus said to this wily foe, "Get thee hence, Satan: for it is written, Thou shalt worship the Lord thy God, and him only shalt thou serve" (Matt. 4:10). Satan had asked Christ to give him evidence that He was the Son of God, and he had in this instance the proof he had asked. At the divine command of Christ he was compelled to obey. He was repulsed and silenced. He had no power to enable him to withstand the peremptory dismissal. He was compelled without another word to instantly desist and to leave the world's Redeemer.

The hateful presence of Satan was withdrawn. The contest was ended. With immense suffering Christ's victory in the wilderness was as complete as was the failure of Adam. And for a season He stood freed from the presence of His powerful adversary, and from his legions of angels.

After Satan had ended his temptations he departed from Jesus for a little season. The foe was conquered, but the conflict had been long and exceedingly trying. And after it was ended Christ was exhausted and fainting. He fell upon the ground as though dying. Heavenly angels who had bowed before Him in the royal courts, and who had been with intense, yet painful, interest watching their loved Commander, and with amazement had witnessed the terrible contest He had endured with Satan, now came and ministered unto Him. *Selected Messages*, Book One, 288.

...Because he [Jesus] had taken upon himself the nature of man, Satan deemed that his victory was certain, and with every malignant device in his power he strove to overcome Christ. The steadfast resistance of Christ to the temptations of the enemy brought the whole confederacy of evil to war against him. Evil men and evil angels united their forces against the Prince of Peace. The issues at stake were beyond the comprehension of men, and the temptations that assailed Christ were as much more intense and subtle than those which assail man as his character was purer and more exalted than is the character of man in his moral and physical defilement. In his conflict with the prince of darkness in this atom of a world, Christ had to meet the whole confederacy of evil, the united forces of the adversary of God and man; but at every point he met the tempter, and put him to flight. Christ was conqueror over the powers of darkness, and took the infinite risk of consenting to war with the enemy, that he might conquer him in our behalf. *The Signs of the Times*, 2-20-93.

When the Saviour finally appeared "in the likeness of men" (Philippians 2:7), and began His ministry of grace, Satan could but bruise the heel, while by every act of humiliation or suffering Christ was bruising the head of His adversary. The anguish that sin has brought was poured into the bosom of the Sinless; yet while Christ endured the contradiction of sinners against Himself, He was paying the debt for sinful man and breaking the bondage in which humanity had been held. Every pang of anguish, every insult, was working out the deliverance of the race. *Prophets and Kings*, 701.

Thank God, we are not left alone. He who "so loved the world, that He gave His only-begotten Son, that whosoever believeth in Him should not perish, but have everlasting life," will not desert us in the battle with the adversary. "Behold," He says, "I give unto you power to tread on serpents and scorpions, and over all the power of the enemy; and nothing shall by any means hurt you." *The Signs of the Times*, 7-27-04.

Satan would cover the people of God with blackness, and ruin them; but Jesus interposes. Although they had sinned, yet Jesus took the guilt of their sins upon his own soul. He snatched the race as a brand from the fire. With his long human arm he encircled humanity, while with his divine arm he grasped the throne of the infinite God. And thus man has strength given him that he may overcome Satan, and triumph in God. Help is brought within the reach of perishing souls; the adversary is rebuked. *Advent Review and Sabbath Herald*, 9-22-96.

The scenes of the past and the future were presented to the mind of Jesus. He beheld Lucifer as he was first cast out from the heavenly places. He looked forward to the scenes of His own agony, when before all the worlds the character of the deceiver should be unveiled. He heard the cry, "It is finished" (John 19:30), announcing that the redemption of the lost race was forever made certain, that heaven was made eternally secure against the accusations, the deceptions, the pretensions, that Satan would instigate. *The Desire of Ages*, 490.

Here are the trophies [those resurrected with Jesus] which Christ took up with Him and presented to the universe of heaven and the worlds that God has created. Any affection that ever they had for Lucifer, who was the covering cherub, is now destroyed. God gave him a chance to work out his character. If He had not done this, there might have been those who felt the accusation he brought against God that He didn't give him a fair chance was justified.

The Prince of Life and the prince of darkness were in conflict. The Prince of Life prevailed, but at an infinite cost. His triumph is our salvation. He is our Substitute and Surety, and what He says to him that overcometh tells whether man has anything to do or not. How? "To him that overcometh will I grant to sit with Me in My throne, even as I also overcame, and am set down with My Father in His throne" (Revelation 3:21). *Faith and Works*, 74.

God had manifested His abhorrence of the principles of rebellion. All heaven saw His justice revealed, both in the condemnation of Satan and in the redemption of man. Lucifer had declared that if the law of God was changeless, and its penalty could not be remitted, every transgressor must be forever debarred from the Creator's favor. He had claimed that the sinful race were placed beyond redemption and were therefore his rightful prey. But the death of Christ was an argument in man's behalf that could not be overthrown. The penalty of the law fell upon Him who was equal with God, and man was free to accept the righteousness of Christ and by a life of penitence and humiliation to triumph, as the Son of God had triumphed, over the power of Satan. Thus God is just and yet the justifier of all who believe in Jesus. . .

In the final execution of the judgment it will be seen that no cause for sin exists. When the Judge of all the earth shall demand of Satan, "Why hast thou rebelled against Me, and robbed Me of the subjects of My kingdom?" the originator of evil can render no excuse. Every mouth will be stopped, and all the hosts of rebellion will be speechless.

The cross of Calvary, while it declares the law immutable, proclaims to the universe that the wages of sin is death. In the Saviour's expiring cry, "It is finished," the death knell of Satan was rung. The great controversy which had been so long in progress was then decided, and the final eradication of evil was made certain. The Son of God passed through the portals of the tomb, that "through death He might destroy him that had the power of death, that is, the devil." Hebrews 2:14. Lucifer's desire for self-exaltation had led him to say: "I will exalt my throne above the stars of God:...I will be like the Most High." God declares: "I will bring thee to ashes upon the earth,...and never shalt thou be any more." Isaiah 14:13, 14; Ezekiel 28:18, 19. When "the day cometh, that shall burn as an oven;...all the proud, yea, and all that do wickedly, shall be stubble: and the day that cometh shall burn them up, saith the Lord of hosts, that it shall leave them neither root nor branch." Malachi 4:1. *The Great Controversy*, 502–504.

Now the guilt of Satan stood forth without excuse. His lying charges against the divine character and government appeared in their true light. He had accused God of seeking merely the exaltation of himself in requiring submission and obedience from his creatures, and had declared that while the Creator exacted self-denial from all others, he himself practiced no self-denial, and made no sacrifice. Now it was seen that for the salvation of a fallen and sinful race, the Ruler of the universe had made the greatest sacrifice which God could make. It was seen, also, that while Lucifer had opened the door for the entrance of sin, by his desire for honor and supremacy, Christ had, in order to destroy sin, humbled himself, and become obedient unto death.

God had manifested his abhorrence of the principles of rebellion. All Heaven saw his justice revealed, both in the condemnation of Satan and in the redemption of man. Lucifer had declared God's law to be of such a character that its penalty could not be remitted, and therefore every transgressor must be forever debarred from the Creator's favor. He had claimed that the sinful race were placed beyond redemption, and were therefore his rightful prey. But the death of Christ was an argument in man's behalf that could not be turned aside. He suffered the penalty of the law. God was just in permitting his wrath to fall upon Him who was equal with himself, and man was set free to accept the righteousness of Christ, and by a life of penitence and humiliation to triumph as the Son of God had triumphed over the power of Satan. *The Spirit of Prophecy*, Volume Four, 322, 323.

There is the throne, and around it the rainbow of promise. There are cherubim and seraphim. The commanders of the angel hosts, the sons of God, the representatives of the unfallen worlds, are assembled. The heavenly council before which Lucifer had accused God and His Son, the representatives of those sinless realms over which Satan had thought to establish his dominion,—all are there to welcome the Redeemer. They are eager to celebrate His triumph and to glorify their King. *The Desire of Ages*, 834.

The power of death was held by the devil; but Jesus had removed its stinging despair, by meeting the enemy upon his own territory and there conquering him. Henceforth death would be robbed of its terror for the Christian, since Christ himself had felt its pangs, and risen from the grave to sit at the right hand of the Father in Heaven, having all power in Heaven and on earth. The conflict between Christ and Satan was determined when the Lord arose from the dead, shaking the prison-house of his enemy to its foundations, and robbing him of his spoils by bringing up a company of the sleeping dead, as a fresh trophy of the victory achieved by the second Adam. This resurrection was a sample, and an assurance, of the final resurrection of the righteous dead at Christ's second coming. *The Spirit of Prophecy*, Volume Three, 239.

A terrible conflict is before us. We are nearing the battle of the great day of God Almighty. That which has been held in control is to be let loose. The angel of mercy is folding her wings, preparing to step down from the throne, and leave the world to the control of Satan. The principalities and powers of earth are in bitter revolt against the God of heaven. They are filled with hatred against those who serve him, and soon, very soon, will be fought the last great battle between good and evil. The earth is to be the battlefield—the scene of the final contest and the final victory. Here, where for so long Satan has led men against God, rebellion is to be forever suppressed. *Advent Review and Sabbath Herald*, 5-13-02.

By his own course of action Satan has forged a chain by which he will be bound. The inhabitants of the heavenly universe will bear witness to God's justice in his destruction. Heaven itself has seen what heaven would be, if he were allowed to remain in it. All the unfallen beings are now united in regarding God's law as changeless. They support the government of Him, who, to redeem the transgressor, spared not His own Son. His law has been proved faultless. His government is forever secure. The Father, the Son, and Lucifer have been revealed in their true relation to one another. God has given unmistakable evidence of His justice and His love. *The Signs of the Times*, 8-27-02.

Chapter 14

SATAN BOUND

The revelator foretells the banishment of Satan and the condition of chaos and desolation to which the earth is to be reduced, and he declares that this condition will exist for a thousand years. After presenting the scenes of the Lord's second coming and the destruction of the wicked, the prophecy continues: "I saw an angel come down from heaven, having the key of the bottomless pit and a great chain in his hand. And he laid hold on the dragon, that old serpent, which is the devil, and Satan, and bound him a thousand years, and cast him into the bottomless pit, and shut him up, and set a seal upon him, that he should deceive the nations no more, till the thousand years should be fulfilled: and after that he must be loosed a little season." Revelation 20:1–3.

That the expression "bottomless pit" represents the earth in a state of confusion and darkness is evident from other scriptures. Concerning the condition of the earth "in the beginning," the Bible record says that it "was without form, and void; and darkness was upon the face of the deep[1]." Genesis 1:2. Prophecy teaches that it will be brought back, partially at least, to this condition. Looking forward to the great day of God, the prophet Jeremiah declares: "I beheld the earth, and, lo, it was without form, and void; and the heavens, and they had no light. I beheld the mountains, and, lo, they trembled, and all the hills moved lightly. I beheld, and, lo, there was no man, and all the birds of the heavens were fled. I beheld, and, lo, the fruitful place was a wilderness, and all the cities thereof were broken down." Jeremiah 4:23–26.

Here is to be the home of Satan with his evil angels for a thousand years. Limited to the earth, he will not have access to other worlds to tempt and annoy those who have never

---

1 The Hebrew word here translated "Deep" is rendered in the Septuagint (Greek) translation of the Hebrew Old Testament by the same word rendered "bottomless pit" in Revelation 20:1–3.

fallen. It is in this sense that he is bound: there are none remaining, upon whom he can exercise his power. He is wholly cut off from the work of deception and ruin which for so many centuries has been his sole delight.

The prophet Isaiah, looking forward to the time of Satan's overthrow, exclaims: "How art thou fallen from heaven, O Lucifer, son of the morning! how art thou cut down to the ground, which didst weaken the nations!...Thou hast said in thine heart, I will ascend into heaven, I will exalt my throne above the stars of God:...I will be like the Most High. Yet thou shalt be brought down to hell, to the sides of the pit. They that see thee shall narrowly look upon thee, and consider thee, saying, Is this the man that made the earth to tremble, that did shake kingdoms; that made the world as a wilderness, and destroyed the cities thereof; that *opened not the house of his prisoners?*" Isaiah 14:12–17.

For six thousand years, Satan's work of rebellion has "made the earth to tremble." He had "made the world as a wilderness, and destroyed the cities thereof." And he "opened not the house of his prisoners." For six thousand years his prison house has received God's people, and he would have held them captive forever; but Christ had broken his bonds and set the prisoners free.

Even the wicked are now placed beyond the power of Satan, and alone with his evil angels he remains to realize the effect of the curse which sin has brought. "The kings of the nations, even all of them, lie in glory, everyone in his own house [the grave]. But thou art cast out thy grave like an abominable branch....Thou shalt not be joined with them in burial, because thou hast destroyed thy land, and slain thy people." Isaiah 14:18–20.

For a thousand years, Satan will wander to and fro in the desolate earth to behold the results of his rebellion against the law of God. During this time his sufferings are intense. Since his fall his life of unceasing activity has banished reflection; but he is now deprived of his power and left to contemplate the part which he has acted since first he rebelled against the government of heaven, and to look forward with trembling and terror to the dreadful future when he must suffer for all the evil that he has done and be punished for the sins that he has caused to be committed. *The Great Controversy*, 658–660.

In the typical service the high priest, having made the atonement for Israel, came forth and blessed the congregation. So Christ, at the close of his work as a mediator, will appear, "without sin unto salvation," [HEB. 9:28] to bless his waiting people with eternal life. As the priest, in removing the sins from the sanctuary, confessed them upon the head of the scapegoat, so Christ will place all these sins upon Satan, the originator and instigator of sin. The scape-goat, bearing the sins of Israel, was sent away "unto a land not inhabited;" [LEV. 16:22.] so Satan, bearing the guilt of all the sins which he has caused God's people to commit, will be for a thousand years confined to the earth, which will then be desolate, without inhabitant, and he will at last suffer the full penalty of sin, in the fires that shall destroy all the wicked. Thus the great plan of redemption will reach its accomplishment in the final eradication of sin, and the deliverance of all who have been willing to renounce evil. *The Great Controversy* [1888 edition], 485, 486.

Now the event takes place foreshadowed in the last solemn service of the Day of Atonement. When the ministration in the holy of holies had been completed, and the sins of Israel had been removed from the sanctuary by virtue of the blood of the sin offering, then the scapegoat was presented alive before the Lord; and in the presence of the congregation the high priest confessed over him "all the iniquities of the children of Israel, and all their transgressions in all their sins, putting them upon the head of the goat." Leviticus 16:21. In like manner, when the work of atonement in the heavenly sanctuary has been completed, then in the presence of God and heavenly angels and the hosts of the redeemed the sins of God's people will be placed upon Satan; he will be declared guilty of all the evil which he has caused them to commit. And as the scapegoat was sent away into a land not inhabited, so Satan will be banished to the desolate earth, an uninhabited and dreary wilderness. *The Great Controversy*, 658.

Chapter 15

SATAN'S END

...We are told of the fall of the angels from their purity, of Lucifer their leader, the instigator of rebellion, of their confederacy and government, of their various orders, of their great intelligence and subtlety, and of their malicious designs against the innocence and happiness of men. We are told of One mightier than the fallen foe, —One by whose authority Satan's power is limited and controlled; and we are told, also, of the punishment prepared for the originator of iniquity. *The Spirit of Prophecy*, Volume Four, 331.

There is no excuse for sin. It will be the final condemnation of Lucifer and his angels that when God shall ask, "Why have ye done this?" they will be able to assign no reason. And when at the last great day sinners are confronted with their sins, and are asked, "Why did you transgress?" every mouth will be stopped. The sinful will stand speechless before God. *Advent Review and Sabbath Herald*, 9-24-01.

It will be in the last great day when every case receives as his works have been; it will be the final and eternal condemnation of the devil and all his sympathizers and all who have served under his jurisdiction and have identified themselves with him. Will he have a reason to assign for his rebellion? When the Judge of all the world demands, Why have ye done thus? what reason can he assign, what cause can he plead? Bear in mind every tongue is silent, every mouth that has been so ready to speak evil, so ready to accuse, so ready to utter words of recrimination and falsehood is stopped, and the whole world of rebellion stands speechless before God; their tongues cleave to the roof of their mouth. The place where sin entered can be specified. *S.D.A. Bible Commentary*, Vol. Four, 1163.

It was seen, also, that while the sin offering pointed to Christ as a sacrifice, and the high priest represented Christ as a mediator, the scapegoat typified Satan, the author of sin, upon whom the sins of the truly penitent will finally be placed. When the high priest, by virtue of the blood of the sin offering, removed the sins from the sanctuary, he placed them upon the scapegoat. When Christ, by virtue of His own blood, removes the sins of His people from the heavenly sanctuary at the close of His ministration, He will place them upon Satan, who, in the execution of the judgment, must bear the final penalty. The scapegoat was sent away into a land not inhabited, never to come again into the congregation of Israel. So will Satan be forever banished from the presence of God and His people, and he will be blotted from existence in the final destruction of sin and sinners. *The Great Controversy*, 422.

"The saints will rest in the Holy City and reign as kings and priests one thousand years; then Jesus will descend with the saints upon the Mount of Olives, and the mount will part asunder and become a mighty plain for the Paradise of God to rest upon. The rest of the earth will not be cleansed until the end of the one thousand years, when the wicked dead are raised, and gather up around the city. The feet of the wicked will never desecrate the earth made new. Fire will come down from God out of heaven and devour them—burn them up root and branch. Satan is the root, and his children are the branches. The same fire that will devour the wicked will purify the earth." *Early Writings*, 51, 52.

All are to hear the last message of warning. The prophecies in the book of Revelation, chapters 12 to 18, are being fulfilled. In the eighteenth chapter is recorded the very last call to the churches. This call is now to be given. In the nineteenth chapter, the time is pictured when the beast and the false prophet are taken and cast into the lake of fire. The dragon, who was the instigator of the great rebellion against heaven, is bound and cast into the bottomless pit for a thousand years. Then follows the resurrection of the wicked and the final destruction of Satan and all the wicked, and the final triumph and reign of Christ in this earth. *Manuscript Releases*, Volume Fifteen, 321, 322.

At last the order to advance is given, and the countless host moves on—an army such as was never summoned by earthly conquerors, such as the combined forces of all ages since war began on earth could never equal. Satan, the mightiest of warriors, leads the van, and his angels unite their forces for this final struggle. Kings and warriors are in his train, and the multitudes follow in vast companies, each under its appointed leader. With military precision the serried ranks advance over the earth's broken and uneven surface to the City of God. By command of Jesus, the gates of the New Jerusalem are closed, and the armies of Satan surround the city and make ready for the onset.

Now Christ again appears to the view of his enemies. Far above the city, upon a foundation of burnished gold, is a throne, high and lifted up. Upon this throne sits the Son of God, and around him are the subjects of his kingdom. The power and majesty of Christ no language can describe, no pen portray. The glory of the Eternal Father is enshrouding his Son. The brightness of his presence fills the city of God, and flows out beyond the gates, flooding the whole earth with its radiance. *The Spirit of Prophecy*, Volume Four, 479.

Satan seems paralyzed as he beholds the glory and majesty of Christ. He who was once a covering cherub remembers whence he has fallen. A shining seraph, "son of the morning;" how changed, how degraded! From the council where once he was honored, he is forever excluded. He sees another now standing near to the Father, veiling His glory. He has seen the crown placed upon the head of Christ by an angel of lofty stature and majestic presence, and he knows that the exalted position of this angel might have been his.

Memory recalls the home of his innocence and purity, the peace and content that were his until he indulged in murmuring against God, and envy of Christ. His accusations, his rebellion, his deceptions to gain the sympathy and support of the angels, his stubborn persistence in making no effort for self-recovery when God would have granted him for-giveness—all come vividly before him. He reviews his work among men and its results—the enmity of man toward his fellow man, the terrible destruction of life, the rise and fall of kingdoms, the overturning of thrones, the long succession of tumults, conflicts, and revolutions. He recalls his constant efforts to oppose the work of Christ and to sink man lower and lower. He sees that his hellish plots have been powerless to destroy those who have put their trust in Jesus. As Satan looks upon his kingdom, the fruit of his toil, he sees only failure and ruin. He has led the multitudes to believe that the City of God would be an easy prey; but he knows that this is false. Again and again, in the progress of the great controversy, he has been defeated and compelled to yield. He knows too well the power and majesty of the Eternal.

The aim of the great rebel has ever been to justify him-self and to prove the divine government responsible for the rebellion. To this end he has bent all the power of his giant intellect. He has worked deliberately and systematically, and with marvelous success, leading vast multitudes to accept his version of the great controversy which has been so long in progress. For thousands of years this chief of conspiracy has palmed off falsehood for truth. But the time has now come when the rebellion is to be finally defeated and the history and character of Satan disclosed. In his last great effort to dethrone Christ, destroy His people, and take possession of the City of God, the archdeceiver has been fully unmasked. Those who have united with him see the total failure of his cause. Christ's followers and the loyal angels behold the full extent of his machinations against the government of God. He is the object of universal abhorrence.

Satan sees that his voluntary rebellion has unfitted him for heaven. He has trained his powers to war against God; the purity, peace, and harmony of heaven would be to him supreme torture. His accusations against the mercy and jus-tice of God are now silenced. The reproach which he has endeavored to cast upon Jehovah rests wholly upon himself. And now Satan bows down and confesses the justice of his sentence.

"Who shall not fear Thee, O Lord, and glorify Thy name? for Thou only art holy: for all nations shall come and worship before Thee; for Thy judgments are made manifest." Verse 4. Every question of truth and error in the long-standing controversy has now been made plain. The results of rebellion, the fruits of setting aside the divine statutes, have been laid open to the view of all created intelligences. The working out of Satan's rule in contrast with the government of God has been presented to the whole universe. Satan's own works have condemned him. God's wisdom, His justice, and His goodness stand fully vindicated. It is seen that all His dealings in the great controversy have been conducted with respect to the eternal good of His people and the good of all the worlds that He has created. "All Thy works shall praise Thee, O Lord; and Thy saints shall bless Thee." Psalm 145:10. The history of sin will stand to all eternity as a witness that with the existence of God's law is bound up the happiness of all the beings He has created. With all the facts of the great controversy in view, the whole universe, both loyal and rebellious, with one accord declare: "Just and true are Thy ways, Thou King of saints."...

Notwithstanding that Satan has been constrained to acknowledge God's justice and to bow to the supremacy of Christ, his character remains unchanged. The spirit of rebellion, like a mighty torrent, again bursts forth. Filled with frenzy, he determines not to yield the great controversy. The time has come for a last desperate struggle against the King of heaven. He rushes into the midst of his subjects and endeavors to inspire them with his own fury and arouse them to instant battle. But of all the countless millions whom he has allured into rebellion, there are none now to acknowledge his supremacy. His power is at an end. The wicked are filled with the same hatred of God that inspires Satan; but they see that their case is hopeless, that they cannot prevail against Jehovah. Their rage is kindled against Satan and those who have been his agents in deception, and with the fury of demons they turn upon them.

Saith the Lord: "Because thou hast set thine heart as the heart of God; behold, therefore I will bring strangers upon thee, the terrible of the nations: and they shall draw their swords against the beauty of thy wisdom, and they shall defile thy brightness. They shall bring thee down to the pit." "I will destroy thee, O covering cherub, from the midst of the stones of fire....I will cast thee to the ground, I will lay thee before kings, that they may behold thee....I will bring thee to ashes upon the earth in the sight of all them that behold thee. ...Thou shalt be a terror, and never shalt thou be any more." Ezekiel 28:6–8, 16–19.

"Every battle of the warrior is with confused noise, and garments rolled in blood; but this shall be with burning and fuel of fire." "The indignation of the Lord is upon all nations, and His fury upon all their armies: He hath utterly destroyed them, He hath delivered them to the slaughter." "Upon the wicked He shall rain quick burning coals, fire and brimstone and an horrible tempest: this shall be the portion of their cup." Isaiah 9:5; 34:2; Psalm 11:6, margin. Fire comes down from God out of heaven. The earth is broken up. The weapons concealed in its depths are drawn forth. Devouring flames burst from every yawning chasm. The very rocks are on fire. The day has come that shall burn as an oven. The elements melt with fervent heat, the earth also, and the works that are therein are burned up. Malachi 4:1; 2 Peter 3:10. The earth's surface seems one molten mass—a vast, seething lake of fire. It is the time of the judgment and perdition of ungodly men—"the day of the Lord's vengeance, and the year of recompenses for the controversy of Zion." Isaiah 34:8.

The wicked receive their recompense in the earth. Proverbs 11:31. They "shall be stubble: and the day that cometh shall burn them up, saith the Lord of hosts." Malachi 4:1. Some are destroyed as in a moment, while others suffer many days. All are punished "according to their deeds." The sins of the righteous having been transferred to Satan, he is made to suffer not only for his own rebellion, but for all the sins which he has caused God's people to commit. His punishment is to be far greater than that of those whom he has deceived. After all have perished who fell by his deceptions, he is still to live and suffer on. In the cleansing flames the wicked are at last destroyed, root and branch—Satan the root, his followers the branches. The full penalty of the law has been visited; the demands of justice have been met; and heaven and earth, beholding, declare the righteousness of Jehovah.

Satan's work of ruin is forever ended. For six thousand years he has wrought his will, filling the earth with woe and causing grief throughout the universe. The whole creation has groaned and travailed together in pain. Now God's creatures are forever delivered from his presence and temptations. "The whole earth is at rest, and is quiet: they [the righteous] break forth into singing." Isaiah 14:7. And a shout of praise and triumph ascends from the whole loyal universe. "The voice of a great multitude," "as the voice of many waters, and as the voice of mighty thunderings," is heard, saying: "Alleluia: for the Lord God omnipotent reigneth." Revelation 19:6. *The Great Controversy*, 669–673.

We invite you to view the complete
selection of titles we publish at:

www.LNFBooks.com

or write or email us your praises,
reactions, or thoughts about this
or any other book we publish at:

TEACH Services, Inc.
P.O. Box 954
Ringgold, GA 30736

info@TEACHServices.com